EXPLORING CAREERS IN COMPUTER GRAPHICS

By

Richard Masterson

THE ROSEN PUBLISHING GROUP
NEW YORK

Published in 1987, 1990 by The Rosen Publishing Group, Inc.
29 East 21st Street, New York, NY 10010

Revised Edition 1990

Library of Congress Cataloging-in-Publication Data

Masterson, Richard.
  Exploring careers in computer graphics.

  Bibliography: p. 155
  Includes index.
  Summary: Explores careers in computer graphics,
describing how to prepare for them and how to find
a job in the field.
    1. Computer graphics—Vocational guidance.
[1. Computer graphics—Vocational guidance.
2. Vocational guidance]   I. Title.
T385.M377   1987   006.6'023   86–28044
ISBN O-8239-1149-7

Manufactured in the United States of America

Acknowledgments

I would like to thank Martin Bressler, Jerry Cahn, Ernie Henrickson, and Giulio Maleci for contributing to this project. By sharing their insight and experience, they reveal part of the "real world" of computer graphics.

I would also like to thank Lucie Curtiss, Josephine Wam, and IBM for generously contributing the illustrations for this book.

Finally, thanks to my graphic arts consultant, Barbara Singer, for her advice and support.

About the Author

Richard Masterson is a Manhattan-based freelance writer. He is currently involved with a new company which uses computers to produce business communications, including graphics.

Contents

Part 1   Overview

I.	*Computer Graphics around You*	3
II.	*Careers in Computer Graphics*	10
III.	*How to Get a Job in Computer Graphics*	15
IV.	*The Technology*	33
V.	*The Microcomputer and the Future*	40
VI.	*Computer Graphics and Your Health*	45

Part 2   Applications

	Introduction	51
VII.	*Art and Animation*	53
VIII.	*CAD/CAM*	61
IX.	*Business*	70

Part 3   Career Profiles

X.	*Interview with a Graphic Design Engineer*	79
XI.	*Interview with a Computer Graphics Entrepreneur*	96
XII.	*Interview with an Educator*	108
XIII.	*Interview with an Analytical Engineer*	118
XIV.	*Interview with a Desktop Publisher*	129

	Appendixes	
A.	*Glossary*	134
B.	*Trade Journals*	137
C.	*Societies and Associations*	138
D.	*Colleges*	140
	Bibliography	155
	Index	156

Part 1
Overview

Chapter 1

Computer Graphics around You

If you've ever played Space Invaders, Pacman, or any other video game, you've already participated in interactive computer graphics. Don't let terms like "interactive computer graphics" throw you; computer graphics isn't something futuristic and arcane that is accessible only to scientific geniuses. In fact, computer graphics is widely used in so many fields that you will probably encounter it if you undertake a career as an architect or an artist, a doctor or a businessman, a pilot or a chemist. People in widely diverse fields employ computer graphics to help them do their jobs more efficiently, more comprehensively. One benefit that users of computer graphics often cite is reward: When you do your job better, you usually find it more personally rewarding.

Computer graphics is here, now. While industry analysts predict a future of dynamic growth in every area across the board, you should realize that computer graphics is already affecting what you see in the world around you. Consider how pervasive the use of computer graphics has become:

A break in the action of Superbowl XVIII, and suddenly a strikingly unique image greets viewers all across America. A gleaming, sexy robotic woman reclines in an easy chair in a futuristic kitchen. She swivels languidly toward the "camera," her sultry voice proclaiming: "Even in the year three thousand, the question still will be: 'What's for dinner?'" She moves an arm, lights a candle with her fingertip, bats her eyes. The first realistic moving character ever produced by computer, she was chosen by the American Can Council to represent their

BRILLIANT IMAGE NEW YORK

product—canned foods. The commercial, created by Robert Abel & Associates for Ketchum Advertising, uses computer graphics to project a contemporary image for canned foods. "We opted for an associative, rather a superrational spot," said Millie Olsen, creative director for Ketchum.

The premium (approximately $500,000) Superbowl media placement heralds the ascendency of computer graphics in television advertising. More and more, advertisers and agencies who want a new, distinctive, imaginative look are turning to computer graphics. Robert Abel & Associates also used computer graphics to create commercials for Levis, TRW, and the Transamerica spot in which King Kong scales the company's building.

When Pepsico management had to decide whether to introduce Slice, a lemon-lime soft drink, in Texas test markets, "business as usual" meant using computer graphics. Computer-generated color-coded maps showing the availability of bottlers versus the competition in key areas provided the indications upon which the decision was made. Slice was successfully introduced in Texas, and subsequently rolled out nationally. The graphics aided Pepsico's management by turning unwieldy reams of computer data into sharp visual references.

Pepsico had committed to acquiring over a quarter of a million dollars worth of decision-support graphics equipment. In 1983 managers produced over 80,000 charts and slides, twenty times as many as in the previous year.

Decision-support computer graphics has become a significant tool throughout the business community, and especially in Fortune 500 companies. General Motors refuses even to discuss its financial decision-support system.

At Brilliant Image, a young New York–based company that creates business graphics on IBM microcomputer systems, president and cofounder Jerry Cahn savors the prospect of unlimited growth potential. A lawyer and psychologist by profession, Jerry saw opportunity in applying microcomputers to produce presentation slides for business. He and his partner had found competitive presentations to be too expensive, too slow in production, and, too often, of pedestrian quality. They founded Brilliant Image to fill this service gap. "At this point I think we're at 0.5 percent of the market," Jerry says; "99.5 percent is still ripe for the plucking."

Computer graphics design, drafting, and manufacturing systems are streamlining architecture and engineering. New York architect Sam Anson Haffey's firm designed a $3 million men's public shelter on Ward's Island in ninety days. Without the computer design system, the project would have taken as much as three times as long. "The speed with which this thing can execute," says Haffey, "is hard to believe."

Michael M. Toby, manager of engineering and computer science for Concourse Engineering Co. in Michigan, a company that offers a variety of mechanical design services, feels committed to using computer systems. "I can see a time, possibly in the next three years," says Toby, "when we will have replaced most of the boards we now have in our drafting room."

Computer design systems are also being applied in medicine.

Dr. Michael Vannier of the Washington University Medical Center, St. Louis, Missouri, helped develop a program that is used mainly for reconstructive facial and orthopedic surgery. Where surgeons used to draw manually on X-rays to plan an operation, now they can plot a precise diagram. Before becoming a radiologist, Dr. Vannier was a NASA engineer.

Behind the scenes at "NBC Nightly News," graphic design engineer Ernie Henrickson works with a Dubner animation system and the Quantel Paint Box to develop graphics ranging from maps and charts to full-scale animations. A first-generation computer artist, Ernie started his career at NBC as a traditional graphic artist. As the network purchased new technology, Ernie learned about each new system—often experimenting on his own—until he became a computer graphics specialist. He says that the computer increases his artistic capability. "You can turn out broadcast quality comps on one of these machines in the time it would take you just to do a pencil sketch at your desk," he says. "They save time; they help my creativity."

At the New York Institute of Technology, Martin Bressler, Art Department chairman and coordinator of the Computer Graphics Program for the Graduate School of Communication Arts, sees the computer as a tool that can extend the artist's reach. "It has opened up a whole new world in the experience of a student who comes from primarily an art background," he says. "If your area is painting, when you use the computer you're suddenly interfacing with video and learning a new language."

Just from this small selection of examples, you can readily see how widely computer graphics is being applied around you—*right now*. Although some applications do smack a little of the esoteric and futuristic, such as jet fighter simulations and NASA animations, the main and growing applications of computer graphics are in the day-to-day operations of business, of engineering, architectural, and manufacturing design, and in the whole spectrum of the graphic arts. The time has already passed when the computer had to prove itself as an effective graphic tool; the task now is to create more new applications that exploit the full potential of computer graphics.

WHAT IS COMPUTER GRAPHICS?

It is difficult to tie "computer graphics" into a tight definition. Essentially, computer graphics refers to any image or images created wholly or partially by a computer. The real meaning of computer graphics resides in each case within the context of a particular application. A bar chart created by a businessman on a personal computer is far different from a full-scale flight simulator, and not really comparable. In every application, however, it must be emphasized that *people* create the graphics. The computer is a powerful tool, but still only a tool. People must initiate the communication that the machine helps to express.

When we speak of computer graphics in the context of careers, we must carefully distinguish between "careers in" and "careers with." For the most part, computer graphics is not a career area in itself. The computer, as a tool, plays a more or less central role in a career, depending on both the function it is required to perform and the knowledge and skill an operator brings to his task. An architect, for example, might design a building exclusively on a CAD system, so his work is entirely "with" computer graphics, but his career still remains "in" architecture. Without his knowledge of architecture, he would be helpless to make use of the computer. The greatest career opportunities, therefore, result from *combined knowledge*: a knowledge of computer graphics and a solid grounding in an applications area.

Computer graphics is divided into three main areas: art/animation, computer-aided design/computer-aided manufacturing (CAD/CAM) and business. These categories should be regarded as descriptive rather than exclusive; some applications can fall under each of the three, and some don't truly fit into any one. They are very useful, however, for grouping similar types of applications, and industry analysts use them to focus on market trends.

1. *Art*

Computers help to produce maps, graphs, charts, and slides

for communication purposes. They are used in package design, advertising art design, and illustration and also to create works of fine art.

Computer-generated animations are increasingly utilized in television for news and weather displays, and in movies and television for a variety of special effects, as well as for the more familiar Disney-type cartoons.

2. *Computer-aided Design/Computer-aided Manufacturing (CAD/CAM)*

As opposed to art, CAD/CAM systems are used for technical design purposes. High-quality printers and plotters help architects and engineers design products ranging from tool bits to jet fighters to apartment complexes. CAD systems offer many benefits for any kind of design and are also utilized in medicine, interior design, and textile design.

3. *Business*

Business employs computer graphics mainly for decision-support and presentation aids in the form of slides, charts,

COMPUTER GRAPHICS PROJECTED GROWTH
TOTAL FIELD
1985-1990
(Billions Of Dollars)

1990 (25.8)

Area Of Greatest Opportunity

1985 (6.2)

Computer graphics will grow at an
annual rate of 32 percent, from 6.2
to 25.8 billion dollars.

graphs, and maps. Artists and service bureaus often produce business graphics; however, the trend is toward internal production on microcomputers.

These areas are discussed in detail in the applications section of this book, where you can see how the computer is actually applied to various real-world tasks. An industry growth outlook is included for each of the three market segments.

On the whole, computer graphics as a field is expected to grow dynamically. The projected growth rate for five years starting in 1985 is *32 percent per year.*

Growth of that magnitude over such a sustained period of time indicates tremendous career opportunities. People will be needed not only in the development and sale of hardware and software, but also in each applications area where the demand originates. If you can utilize the new technology, you have a potent skill to offer when you enter the job market.

Chapter II

Careers in Computer Graphics

Is there a career for you in computer graphics?

Almost definitely. Computer graphics is applied in such a diverse range of fields that rewarding career opportunities exist for many kinds of people. This diversity in itself indicates a broad range of career opportunity, but it is impossible to over-state the significance of the industry's explosive growth rate. People are carried right along with this growth: Not only does it cause demand for people with computer graphics knowledge at

the entry level, but it also propels able people rapidly up the career ladder. The field is still so young and vigorous that you may find yourself teaching what you learned in your first year to several new people in your second. If you're good, before you know it you will be designing your own projects, managing groups of people junior to you, and making a sizable income.

If you are a student looking for the area of greatest opportunity, computer graphics is it; if you are a wife and mother and want a career where you won't feel as if you're starting from behind, computer graphics is for you. If you're an artist looking for a new way to express yourself and make money, you're looking for computer graphics; if you ultimately want to own your own business, computer graphics is your springboard. If your interest is in architecture or engineering or any kind of design, computer graphics is the tool you need. If you want to get in the fast lane in business, computer graphics will help you make decisions faster and persuade more compellingly. If you want a career that gives you continual growth opportunity as well as personal and financial rewards, computer graphics is for you.

The mere fact that you've acquired this book and begun turning the pages suggests that you may be the kind of person who would do extremely well in computer graphics. If you recognize yourself in one or more of the following criteria, computer graphics is a field you can do well in and, more important, a field in which you can enjoy doing well.

You:

-are curious
-enjoy communicating visually
-are creative
-have a flair for design
-are entrepreneurial
-enjoy making presentations
-like computers

Aggressiveness is one character trait that seems to apply particularly strongly to computer graphics. If you are willing to continually take on new challenges, to keep right on top of emerging technology in your applications area, to experiment and find new ways of doing things, to work at being a leader throughout your career, then you will flourish in computer graphics.

Don't think that "aggressive" means "overbearing," "selfish," or "pushy." Aggressiveness also refers to confidence in ability, to a willingness to confront unknowns and solve problems without being intimidated. It is a positive trait discernible in even the shyest people when it refers to this kind of confident intellectual attitude. If you like what you do and continue to pursue it, you can rise to career success almost effortlessly. When your interests coincide with the growth of the industry, you don't have to separate advancing your career from conducting your normal day-to-day activity.

If you don't feel that you possess this kind of aggressiveness, if you really just want to learn to function, perform it responsibly, and pick up a check at the end of the week, stay away from computer graphics. Not only will you find yourself continually passed over for promotion in favor of younger, aggressive movers who are at the cutting edge of the technology, but you may also find that your failure to keep up will render you obsolescent. In CAD/CAM, for example, Edward McAlpin, director of computer graphics for Time Engineering in Troy, Michigan, reports that " ... analyses have shown that college graduates out of school for only seven years who have not taken postgraduate courses are currently obsolete."

You will have to be aggressive even when pursuing your education. Most schools have far more students than computers; computer time tends to be expensive. So computer time is limited and competitive. Professor Bressler of NYIT says that students' greatest frustration is that "they don't get enough time on the computer." You will usually have to complete your assignments in set amounts of time; you may often have to compete with fellow students for extra time for special projects. You may find yourself working with someone literally looking over your shoulder, waiting for a chance, hoping to get some of your time. To do well, you will have to be confident that you can execute your assignments within stipulated time limits.

If you can handle that kind of pressure comfortably, you're well suited to a career in computer graphics. Traditional graphics education doesn't always expose students to the kinds of pressure they will receive when they go to work. The pressure inherent in computer education gives, as Professor Bressler says, "some very relevant, real-world experience."

A last note on aggressiveness: When it comes to getting a job, the pushy kind doesn't hurt. Getting that all-important first job can often be a direct function of how many doors you knock on. If you knock on twenty doors, you have twenty chances to be hired; if you knock on one hundred, you have one hundred; if you commit yourself to a thorough, determined effort, the number of your possible opportunities becomes infinite. Once you are launched in your field, however, it is your skills that determine your future.

Computer graphics technology brings change. It imperils the very existence of some occupations and will forever change the normal operation of others. It has already exhibited the capacity to assume the functions of:

  -architectural draftsmen;
  -animation mainframe inbetweeners;
  -mechanical (pasteup) artists.

Many of the companies already using computer systems for graphic art production report that they have been able to reduce their graphic arts staff or to realize increases in productivity without employing more artists. In addition, the computer makes it possible for less-skilled, lower-paid employees to replace artists in the production of standard or repetitive materials. For instance, where an artist might have prepared a weekly chart reflecting a company's sales performance, with the computer a secretary can simply input the updated figures and let the preformatted computer program do the rest.

Artists in the video and film production industries can uniformly expect exposure to computer systems. The computer provides a direct interface to video; actual video images can be frozen and modified. If you want to get involved in the video industry, plan on working on paint and animation systems. The days of filming graphics off of boards for editing into programs are numbered.

In CAD/CAM applications the computer is enabling existing

staffs to achieve greater productivity. Its ability to produce high-quality drawings right from the original design eliminates the need for redrawing, or drawing to specifications, as the architectural draftsman does. The computer also has the capacity to work around the clock. Companies wishing to recoup the sizable investment in a CAD system, to meet production deadlines, or to increase productivity can go to two- and three-shift days.

The computer is making inroads into engineering design and manufacturing at a great pace. Prospective engineers and architects can't afford much computer resistance: If you want to go into one of these design areas, you should assume that you'll be sitting in front of a CAD system before the end of your career.

If you *don't* want to get involved with computer graphics, tread with care in the above areas.

If you're interested in innovation, growth, and finding new ways to communicate, you're moving in the same direction as computer graphics. Computer graphics is a young, vigorous industry that needs people with vision, people who are willing to put in all the hard work required to realize that vision. It's not for imitators, bureaucrats, or lackeys. Something over 80 percent of normal business entails the maintenance and repetition of standard operations; computer graphics is moving too fast to become clogged with that kind of organizational sludge. But it offers great promise to anyone who is willing and able to keep up with the pace.

Chapter **III**

How to Get A Job in Computer Graphics

Decide early. The earlier you decide on a career area, the better. The more specifically you define your career goals, the better. Only after you decide what job you want can you begin to position yourself to get it. If your interest centers on a general area, you can make concrete moves toward preparing yourself to enter that area. If you feel that you can precisely identify the position you eventually want to obtain, you can begin to accumulate the necessary credentials and even to garner some of the "extras" that set you apart from the competition. Eventually, you will have to specify a job, with the attendant title, duties, and salary level. You cannot seek employment before you have positioned yourself to fill a specific, existing job. The earlier you choose your direction, the easier it will be to position yourself successfully.

The decision process is extremely difficult, entailing frustrating false starts and wasted time, but the stakes are high. You will probably spend the majority of the waking hours of your adult life working at your job. And, almost ironically, when you find work enjoyable and rewarding, you will tend to perform better and realize more income to spend in your leisure time than you would if you didn't like your job. Your job affects your life—even when you're not working.

Far too many people fail to make a viable career choice, or fail to recognize the importance of making one before it is too late. After they finish their education, their direction becomes ambiguous. They are buffeted by coincidence until inertia drives them into a career-by-accident. Few are those lucky enough to find inertia's choice one they can live happily with for the rest of their lives. A good place to begin looking for a career in computer graphics that's right for you is the applications section of this book (Part 2). Read about where and how computer graphics is being applied, and also about salary levels and the outlook for the future. Once you've discovered an area that attracts you, it's time to learn more. Talk to friends about what they're doing and what they've found out; can you learn anything by comparing their goals to yours? Talk to your parents, and have your parents talk to their friends. If you get all the people you know helping you, you should be able to contact someone who works in the field and can really fill you in. If you're lucky, you may find a mentor, someone who will advise you through your development, your first job hunt, and your career progression. You should also read trade journals (Appendix B). Trade journals are directed at a specific industry community and can give you a good idea about the main concerns of that industry. They can also clue you in on salary levels and life-style concerns such as hours, pressures, and mobility. Finally, try to get on the system you think you'll eventually be using. This may be difficult, but it's worth a little extra effort; you'll get an honest gut feeling when you sit in front of the real thing.

Once you've selected a specific career goal and digested your impression of the life-style it would offer, you've completed the most difficult part of launching your career. Now that you know where you want to go, you can begin taking the individual steps that will get you there.

THE RÉSUMÉ

The résumé is a profound document. It is a one-page review of your training and experience that is intended to induce an employer to call you in for a serious job interview. When you get that interview, most of the questions you are asked will be derived from your résumé. To get a good job, you must have a good résumé.

Ideally, your résumé will display an excellent educational record, several years of directly related employment experience, and perhaps even an item of compelling human interest. When you're just starting a career you obviously don't have the experience. But your résumé can indicate that you are knowledgeable about specific systems, that you are capable of fulfilling the duties of the position you are applying for, that you are the kind of person a company can confidently invest in.

The two main areas you need to cover on your résumé are educational background and work experience. You should be aware of the need to fill these categories long before you begin seeking your first career job. If you have a good background and some experience, you shouldn't have any trouble writing your résumé. If you don't, filling that one piece of paper will be an arduous task, the completion of which won't satisfy you.

Getting the right education is your first priority. In general, you want to establish a strong academic record at the best school you can manage to attend. For computer graphics, you want a school that has a strong department in your applications area and that also offers experience with the systems currently in professional use. This can be tricky: Some schools insist that they offer the training you need, even though their systems are out of date. They aren't lying, for in a loose sense all computer graphics are related, and any experience is better than none. But that sense is too loose for you. The technology is susceptible to rapid evolution. You must stay in touch with technological developments in the marketplace. Read the trade journals, and try to find someone in the field to help you keep informed.

Another problem is deciding between a school that is strong in your applications area and one that is strong in computer graphics. There are two schools of thought on this problem. The first holds that creative skills take precedence over technical experience. Computer graphics is so new that companies will expect to train you; they will hire you purely for your design ability. The second school of thought holds that because computer graphics is so new, companies place a premium on people with system-specific experience. They will hire you if you can begin to produce immediately, rather than because you have a high cume.

There is something to be said for each of these schools of thought. If you are forced to decide between a top-level college that is weak in computer graphics and a middle-level school that is strong in computer graphics, choose the top school. Having a top school on your résumé sets you above the pack; you should acquire this premium, and then direct your free time toward gaining a high level of computer experience. This holds especially true if you plan to go to a graduate school where you can obtain comparable computer training. Also, it's easier to win an internship and gain some experience in a company when you come from a top school.

If you don't get into a top school, think about focusing more strongly on the computer aspect of your education. You will eventually have to compete with people from the top schools; you can set yourself apart from them by exhibiting strong system-specific experience. While you should never let your cume slip, pursue courses you can apply even if it means passing up easy "A" courses.

Consider pursuing a double major, or a minor to go with your major. A major generally takes up only about one third of your total undergraduate course work, so you may be able to accumulate the credits for a second major or a minor without unduly taxing yourself. Don't go for more than you can handle, however; two shoddy degrees can't measure up to one good one.

The second most likely area to explore is computer science. Even coupled with a fine arts degree, a computer science degree lends an extra impression of competence. For the more technical and specialized areas, the added concentration becomes even more valuable. If you want to apply computer graphics in medicine, for example, you will probably want both a computer science degree and a medical degree. Conversely, if you are interested in computer science and want to get involved with graphics, you should consider training in an applications area.

Some schools allow a student to design his own interdisciplinary minor or to modify the requirements for his major. If you see a viable way to combine computer graphics with your applications area, or to initiate a special project on your own, consult with your faculty adviser and see about getting credit for what you want to do. A school's primary function is to serve students; you have every right to request the individualized curriculum that suits you best.

Investigate all scholarships for which you are eligible. Even if you aren't financially needy, any scholarship you earn on merit will enhance your résumé. Although you are unlikely to find scholarships specifically in computer graphics, each applications area offers opportunities to earn scholarships that you can also apply to your computer graphics work.

Get involved in some extracurricular activities to flesh out your personality. At worst, they will show that you are willing to do things on your own time and that you can function effectively in groups. At best, they will show a serious accomplishment, indicating that you possess initiative and leadership qualities. When you mention some of your personal interests on your résumé, you give your prospective employer a broader way to relate to you.

Whereas the paths toward advanced education are well traveled and easy to discern, the trail that leads to an advantageous part-time or summer job can be hard to find. However, you need to show some experience on your résumé. Even general employment experience indicates that you have exposure to the world of commerce and that you can be relied on to the extent of your duties. If constraints such as the need for money or geographical isolation make it impossible for you to find a job that ties in to your career area, your résumé can still stress the responsibility you shouldered and the unique perspective you gained through your general employment.

The work that really pays off big, however, is work in your career field. Perhaps the best, most available way to get work-in-field is to obtain an internship. Many people become stubbornly shortsighted when it comes to working; they want money. When you put an internship into the context of a smooth career development and its material benefits, it is of incomparably greater value than the money you might have made during the same period of time at some kind of irrelevant labor. Companies generally expose interns to a broad view of the business as well as some specific hands-on work. This kind of training not only makes for an excellent résumé entry but can also open a big door for you. Companies don't grant internships out of an overpowering altruistic impulse—they want to develop the best young talent they can find. You should get a chance at a job in the company you intern with, and you will also be in a perfect position to make valuable personal contacts with professionals already working in the field.

Internships at good companies are highly competitive. To get one, you need to take exactly the same steps as you would searching for your first job. If you can't find one after an initial search, don't give up. Since most internships are given during the summer, you might consider taking a semester off from school and interning in the fall or spring. Also, you can try to persuade a company that doesn't have a program to start one with you. The offer of a free and willing pair of hands is hard to turn down. Even if you're a twenty-two-year-old college senior, don't turn down an invaluable chance at real experience just because it doesn't offer money.

The typewriter offers entrée to the business environment. If you can type fifty words per minute, you can do office temporary work and possibly get into a company you are interested in. Typing your way into a company is not as good as interning; you will spend most of your time working at repetitive tasks rather than training. However, you can pick up a lot of useful information along the way, you can make contacts, and you will be paid. Typing is a worthwhile skill. If you type you can produce better-looking papers in less time, which can't hurt your grades; you can produce more, better-looking cover letters and other correspondence for your job search; and you will also be comfortable when you approach a computer keyboard.

When you're coming into computer graphics from another career you have less opportunity to orchestrate your development; however, the steps you should take are essentially the same. Education is available in night courses, and occasionally in concentrated summer courses that you might be able to fit in during a vacation. For experience, you should try to direct your current occupation to partake in at least some aspect of the applications area you want to enter. If something in your present job has stimulated your interest in computer graphics, that may not be too difficult. If you are making a more radical career shift, be prepared to take a long-range view of the transition. Properly positioning yourself for a new career takes time. One thing you should do is consider the mobility available in your present area: Try to engineer some connection with the career you want to start. A change of responsibilities or geographic location in your present career area could prove beneficial for your eventual crossover. When you do go for the new job, the more consistent your development looks on your résumé, the better.

ARTHUR I. DESIGN
2528 Broadway 6B
New York, New York 10025
(212) 666-6500

EXPERIENCE

7/84–Present: **Compuvision Corporation**   Hartford, CT
Junior Designer
Design sales brochures, advertising, corporate identity. Work on DEC, Harris computers with Quantel Paintbox system. Responsible for projects from concept to finished production.

6/83–9/83 **Smart Productions**   Brooklyn, NY
Production Assistant
Assisted with all facets of corporate slide presentation. Designed unique bar and pie charts on IBM PC AT.

6/82–9/82 **Smart Productions**   Brooklyn, NY
Intern
Responsible for administrative tasks, including client contact.

EDUCATION

1983 **New York Institute of Technology**   New York, NY
Master of Fine Arts. Designed on Images I and Images II paint systems. Utilized fractal geometry for design applications. Responsible for graduate video workshop.

6/81–9/81 **School of Visual Arts**   New York, NY
Completed intensive microcomputer (Apple IIe) graphic design course.

1981 **Rhode Island School of Design**   Newport, RI
B.F.A. Graphic design, printmaking, computer graphics. Created diverse color images on Apple Macintosh microcomputer.

OTHER Captain, Rhode Island School of Design fencing team.

Member, National Computer Graphics Association.

References On request.

Your résumé should scan easily so that the person reading it can quickly ascertain your name, the position you are applying for, and the relevant data about your background.

Your name goes on the top center, followed by your address and phone number. If you are not at home during business hours and don't have a phone answering machine, consider leaving another number where a message can be left for you. Skip several lines and write either "Position" or "Objective" in capital letters, followed by a colon, at the left margin. Move in about 10 spaces and write in the title of the position you will be applying for. An accurate one-word description is best, but a more general objective statement is acceptable. Avoid grandiose posturing such as: "... and eventually become chairman of the board." You can show ambition, but temper it with realism.

You should now maintain the two-column format, with the category title at the left margin and your information lining up with the first letter of your position description. Space three lines and write in either "Experience" or "Education." If you have some good experience, lead with it. If your education says more good things about you, lead with that. Place appropriate dates under category titles at the left margin. In general, double-space between entries within a category, and triple-space between categories. If your résumé is a little long or short, adjust your spacing and margins accordingly. Don't use more than one page unless you have enough professional experience to mandate two.

Under "Experience," list your jobs in reverse chronological order, the most recent first. Place the dates during which you worked at the left margin. If you are currently employed, write "Present" rather than a closing date. Use the physical size of your entries to help give the impression that you have been consistently developing throughout your career. Make the most recent the longest, most detailed entry, and make the oldest entry quite terse.

Under "Education" list only your graduation dates. If you spent a little extra time graduating, that's your business alone. Don't include high school unless you have some major accomplishment to report. Professional education really starts with college.

After "Experience" and "Education"—the real meat of your

résumé—you can enter another category to include any other accomplishments that recommend you. This is where you can say that you were captain of a club or a sports team, that you are a Cordon Bleu chef, that you participate in a charitable organization. Use this category to flesh out your personality a little and make yourself interesting.

For the last item on your résumé, write "References" at the margin, and "Available on request" in the right column. If you have a portfolio, indicate it with a little emphasis by writing "Portfolio" at the left margin and "Available on request" in the right column.

Use the most active language possible to describe your accomplishments. Say "created, designed, initiated, produced, and responsible for." Display yourself in a positive light. Never lie, but don't be shy about taking full credit for any project you participated in or maximizing its importance. Specifically mention every piece of equipment you've worked on, and make sure that you sound familiar with it.

The present tense gives an active impression, so use it for your present job description. Your presence in your job descriptions is understood, so omit the "I."

Be sure your résumé looks professional. The best way to ensure this is to have it printed on bond paper. If you feel that you may want to make a lot of changes or that the expense involved in printing is too great, you can type it on a good typewriter or word processor and then photocopy it on bond paper.

THE COVER LETTER

When you mail your résumé you will need to include a cover letter. The cover letter allows you much more latitude than the résumé. You are free from the restrictions of chronology and job description and can introduce any information that you feel reflects positively on you. The cover letter should complement your résumé: Together they should make you appear perfect for the job. A well-written cover letter forces a reader to focus on the most pertinent and most impressive aspects of the résumé it accompanies.

Your cover letter should look professional. Consult a style

manual if you're unsure about business letter format. Check your grammar and spelling, and then have someone else proofread the letter for you. Sloppiness or inattention to details like proper word division could cost you an interview. After all the work you've done up to this point, don't let a simple typo ruin a potential opportunity.

Your letter must be specific. People recognize form letters and consign them to the trash without compunction. When they receive a letter that's personally addressed to them and shows some knowledge of and interest in their company, however, they will pay honest attention. Always mail your letter to a specific person. A simple phone call can get you the name of the appropriate person, and his title. Try to mention something specific about the company that ties in to your reason for writing. This might be an article in a trade magazine reporting on some aspect of the company or business that interests you.

Don't permit any negatives in your letter. Even if you can reconcile something in your résumé that you think might be considered negative, it's better not to mention it at all than to draw your reader's attention to it and risk having him dwell on it. You do have to explain a major résumé problem; if you have a five-year gap between jobs, you need to assure a potential employer that you weren't in prison during that time—even if you were! Otherwise, you should assume a very positive tone. Use lots of strong, active verbs; emphasize your accomplishments and display some enthusiasm about the possibility of working for the company. They really do want you to care. Mention the specific system the company uses; if you've never worked on it, mention it twice. The cover letter is the place to tell someone how really good you are, but use discretion and good taste; you don't want to sound as if you are bragging.

You may occasionally answer ads in classified sections of newspapers. Some of these are blind ads that give only a box number for replies. Companies use blind ads to avoid being deluged with inquiries from job-hunters. So don't get lazy when you answer a classified ad just because you don't see the name of a desirable company under it. In many cases the company is so desirable that it wishes to remain anonymous. Be sure to address the ad specifically; supply all the information it requests. According to personnel directors, job-hunters frequently fail to deliver what an ad asks for. If you don't read the ad carefully, you're probably wasting your time answering it at all. Don't, however, supply salary information. It is illegal for a company to check on a salary history; you probably won't have one yet anyway, but you are never required to supply one. Don't cite a salary requirement either, unless you wouldn't take the job without a high salary, for instance, for geographical considerations. Especially at entry level, you are likely to get a more or less standard wage, and you may get more by waiting for an offer than by supplying a requirement.

A cover letter has three basic parts: an introduction, the body of the letter, and a closing in which you attempt to establish further contact. The introduction establishes your reason for writing—your interest in the company. Try to mention specific names, dates, and numbers. "*Computer Pictures*' March 1986 article 'The Design of the Future' reports that General Computing intends to produce 20 percent more real time animations..." Or, "John Wiley, VP Marketing at ACI, recommended that I contact you..." Names, dates, and numbers look impressive and are impossible to disagree with. Use them to appear professional and up-to-date.

The body of the letter develops your interest in the company and discusses your suitability for employment. Emphasize your qualifications, and don't be afraid to draw conclusions for your reader: "As you can see from my résumé..." The body usually consists of two to four paragraphs in a standard, one-page letter. If you want to write a longer letter—and you have something to say and the ability to communicate it in writing— go for a really long letter. If you can hold your reader's attention for five pages, you've already established a rapport. In general, you'll want to go with the standard one-page letter because the longer ones are difficult and time-consuming to produce. If you do go longer, try to avoid a two-page letter. Two-page letters usually look as if they should have been condensed into one.

Call for action in the last paragraph of your letter. The letter to this point works to get your toe in the door. Don't now say "Thank you" and just back away— walk right in! Say, "I will call you on Monday, February 3, at 10 a.m. to set up an interview." Or, "I will be in the city to show my portfolio during the week of February 3. I will call on Friday, January 9, to confirm which day will be best for you to see it." If you are good enough, say "You call me." Let your reader know that you are confident and capable: Call for action.

Creative Strategies

If you are pursuing a creative occupation, you may want to demonstrate your creativity in your cover letter. For example, if you want to be an advertising art director, it would be appropriate for your cover letter to be an ad, with yourself as the product. In general, the résumé is not the place for creativity; just from its look and feel, it should say professional. The letter, on the other hand, can go on to demonstrate some of what you really can do. If you include a computer image and discuss how you created it, your reader may be inclined to regard you as an actual artist rather than as a potential one.

Don't choose a creative appeal if you have a strong résumé. When you already expect to be able to get interviews, there's no point in introducing complications, especially when they involve another person's taste.

Do choose a creative appeal if you don't feel that your résumé is outstanding, or if the field is so competitive that it's difficult to get interviews anyway. It's usually hard to get attention when you are trying to enter a creative field; a creative cover letter is one way to get someone interested in you.

Creative approaches are always risky because they depend on personal taste. While you may interest some people who share your taste, you may alienate others entirely. Be sure you're good enough. To make any headway with a creative approach, you're going to have to impress working professionals with your ability. Something that was a hit in your school paper might not work in this tougher arena. Bear in mind that you're always better off using a standard letter than sending a creative one that falls short of the mark.

Consider whether your cover letter complements your portfolio. Does it provoke interest in the work that you will show to follow it? Is it of the same high standard? You will also want to ascertain whether you are achieving more with the cover letter than you would by simply including a sample from your portfolio. It's better to show your portfolio as a whole when you interview and can present it in person, but if you feel that a sample would attract more interest than any letter you might contrive, send one. There are no hard and fast rules here; you can send both the letter and one or more samples, or even your whole portfolio, if you can afford the postage. Finally, be sure that whatever you decide to include copies well as a photostat or a xerographic copy.

After you decide what to send, there are a lot of ways of getting it there. Regular mail is the usual way, but you can devise any number of schemes to get extra attention and, hopefully, favorable reactions. People have sent résumés printed on T-shirts, in boxes of pizza, in bags containing coffee and donuts, and by messenger delivery. You can have your résumé blown up and mounted on a board so that it won't even fit in a trash can if someone wants to throw it out, or in a filing cabinet if they want to bury it. If you let your imagination go, you may be able to make people so curious that they will call you for an interview just to see what you're really like. Do follow the restraints of good taste, however, for the line between the creative and the obnoxious is very thin at times.

The bottom line on the creative approach: When your portfolio is great and your résumé is weak, try it; when you haven't been successful with standard methods, try it; when you're so good that your scheme can't fail, go for it.

WHERE TO LOOK

You don't have to have completed your résumé before you start thinking about where you might like to work. In fact, the more information you have about the type of company you want to work for, the more effectively you can direct your résumé. After you have completed your résumé, however, you'll be ready to start your job search and you'll need to compile a list of companies to contact.

Go to the library. Most full-service libraries have both a career section and a business section. Perhaps the most valuable resource you will find in these sections in the librarian. Librarians are there specifically to help you, and they will know how to locate most of the information you will need about fields and companies. Your school's career guidance office may be able to provide you with most of the library's functions. Consult them to find out which companies recruit your school; you may be able to set up an interview right there, and you can expect to be well received by those companies anyway.

Consult Appendix B for an appropriate trade journal in which you can find articles about companies and people in your field. Many of these publications also carry classified sections. While you're unlikely to find many ads for entry-level applicants, you can get an idea about which companies are hiring. In general, companies that are growing usually have the most openings, so watch for them as you read. Appendix C lists societies and associations that can provide you with valuable information on various areas of computer graphics. The National Computer Graphics Association (NCGA) and the Association for Computing Machinery's Special Interest Group on Computer Graphics (SIGGRAPH) hold regular conventions in various geographical locations.

The hottest tips often come from word of mouth, so make all your relatives and friends aware that you are in the job market and interested in any leads. Get in the habit of reading the weekly business section in your Sunday paper. The New York *Times*, for instance, has a whole recruitment division in its business section. It lists jobs throughout the country. This is where you will find announcements about conventions and expositions being held by companies or associations. You should also read the business section to stay informed about the economic trends that affect the economy in general and your industry in particular. That will help you sound smart when you interview.

After you've gone through all the steps—consulted your career guidance office, your friends and family, appropriate associations, societies, directories, magazines, and newspapers—you are ready to go out and get that job.

HOW TO LOOK

You now have a list of companies that you are prepared to solicit for employment. The length of your list depends on your rough estimation of your chances—somewhere between 20 and 100; perhaps even more for highly competitive positions. Your objective is to get as many interviews as you can, with interviews for live jobs taking precedence over exploratory interviews.

A common, easy, and wrong method of contacting companies is simply to stuff the mailbox with résumés and then sit at home waiting for the phone to ring. That is tantamount to throwing your destiny to the wind and washing your hands of any further responsibility. You will end up mailing résumés, but the first thing you should do is get on the phone yourself. Call every company on your list, asking first whether there is a current opening, second whether they expect to hire at that level in the near future, and third the name and title of the person to whom you should send a résumé. This is a lot harder than it sounds: You will get confused answers from new secretaries, you will be connected to the wrong person, you will be put on hold and hung up on repeatedly. But don't be discouraged; believe it or not, this is just normal business communication. Be firm, polite, and persistent.

Three things can result from your phone search. The best is that you actually get a live interview and bypass writing entirely. You owe it to yourself to take a shot at getting hired right off before you become involved in the labor-intensive writing process. Many companies will refuse to give you information over the phone, or will tell you that the standard procedure is to send in a résumé and will give you the name and title of the person to contact. The last thing you may find out is that the company doesn't hire at your level at all, which means you can simply cross them off your list and not spend any further effort.

Conduct your search in *reverse* alphabetical order. Most people compile their lists in alphabetical order, the order that they copy from books. By going in reverse order, you increase your chances of reaching companies that haven't already been inundated with applications.

Be prepared to ask for an interview when you call, and be ready to summarize your background and ask for an interview when you get to speak to a person who is responsible for hiring. If you don't like to ad lib, write out a short paragraph about your background that you can read over the phone.

Ideally, your telephone search will yield some interviews. In any case, however, it will give you your next list to pursue: the names and titles to address. When you write, give precedence to the jobs you think are live, and to managers over personnel directors. Don't try to get it all done at once. Write a focused, researched cover letter for each company. You will find that the calling phases and the writing phases of your search coincide. In a typical day of searching you may make twenty-five calls, actually contact ten people, and decide on five people to write to. Even one interview represents an excellent day's work.

Whenever possible, contact managers rather than personnel directors. Managers make the ultimate hiring decisions; personnel has the authority to turn you down but can only recommend you for hiring. In many cases, a personnel department will check a list for openings, and if there aren't any, will simply file your résumé. Personnel departments can also have certain vested interests. If they have invested time and money recruiting from certain schools, they're unlikely to consider you if you don't fill an immediate need. A manager, on the other hand, usually has the authority to tell personnel to hire you next, or even to create an opening specifically for you.

When you're sending a creative cover letter, you especially need to find a manager. Personnel is interested in *quantity*; they like to see a list of "impeccable credentials." A manager is more interested in *quality*; he is responsible for actually producing and cares about what you can do now. If your portfolio grabs him, he won't care where you've been before.

Finding the right manager to contact can be difficult. In general, you want someone who is high enough to be powerful but not so high that he is inaccessible. He will tend to be a vice president, but not an executive vice president. Look for managers in industry directories, in the editorial matter in trade publications. You can also call companies direct and ask who is in charge of a certain project. Just because you've already contacted personnel doesn't mean that you can't go on to contact a manager.

THE INTERVIEW

Interviews are of two kinds: live and exploratory. Emphasize live interviews, but take every opportunity to go on exploratory interviews. Exploratory interviews occur when a company has no position presently available but is still willing to speak to you, and when you make personal contact with people working in the field. Exploratory interviews can pay off directly when a company is impressed enough to remember you when the next opening comes up, or when a personal contact feels strongly enough to recommend you. They can pay off in two other, equally important ways. First, you will gain valuable experience at interviewing; you can get comfortable in the interview situation without having to be concerned about possible rejection. Second, the exploratory interview is an ideal place to get leads: ask your interviewer for advice. He knows you want to enter the field and that he doesn't have anything immediate to offer you. But the one thing he can do is pick up the phone and arrange to have other people he knows in the field see you. One exploratory interview can generate three more interviews, one of which might be live.

When you get to that live interview, it's time for all the preparation you've done to pay off. Make sure that you cover all the bases. Dress professionally and conservatively. Gray is an exciting color for an interview. Shine your shoes, clean your nails, and put your hair under control. If you smoke, don't, and deny that you ever have. Personnel directors will actually check on all these things—they want to see that you understand and are willing to play by the rules. Leave your creativity in your portfolio and dress like a banker going to a funeral. You can come in wearing your old jeans *after* you get the job.

An interview is basically an exchange of information between two people, but there are several keys to interviewing well. The first is that you must ask questions. Even if you are sure that you want the job and there's nothing further that you need to know, you can't afford merely to answer your interviewer's questions. Ask what your specific duties will be, what the worst problems are, what the next step in your career progression would be. Find out about the people you would be working with. Ask about the company's culture, and what it is most proud of. You want to appear alive and intelligent; it also doesn't hurt if it seems that you're evaluating the company against several other strong possibilities. Asking questions will also help you to establish a dialogue. Get your interviewer thinking; you will have a more profitable and memorable exchange.

Appear enthusiastic. Even when the job entails some drudgery or dues-paying, don't be honest. Don't say, "The first year will be a drag, but eventually I'll get to do what I really want." Say things like, "Everyone has to pay his dues" and, "I'm sure there's a lot to be learned." Companies really like that little extra bit of positive attitude. Saying, "I really want to work here at General Computing" could be the factor that makes them decide on you instead of someone else with virtually the same credentials.

Memorize your résumé. You will be questioned on it, and you don't ever want to appear confused. Instead, be prepared to say something interesting about each entry. Knowing your résumé will help you establish a strong first impression.

Avoid negatives. You want to leave behind a very positive impression, so don't bring up problems, even if they have been well reconciled. Don't volunteer any information that is uncomplimentary to you. If you do have a gap in your qualifications, try to avoid discussing it. Change the subject by asking questions or redirecting your interviewer to your résumé. Last, try to emphasize your strongest point. When the interviewer remembers you after seeing a dozen other people, you want him to focus on your best quality. You want him to think, "He was the one with all that Autocad experience." Make your best quality a stand-out that will be remembered. Discuss it. Repeat it.

ONWARD AND UPWARD

Make your first job a career springboard. Come to work early, stay late, take on all the responsibility you can get. If you're tabbed as an early comer, your climb up the ladder will be all that much faster and easier. Try to work under the best senior person in the company, and learn everything he knows. You will have to continually learn about new technological developments to stay in computer graphics; try to become the one to whom all the others turn for the latest word. You can preempt part of the mystique of powerful new technologies just by keeping up on your reading.

Finally, set realistic goals for yourself. You don't necessarily want to head a multinational conglomerate. In the end, the whole point boils down to whether you enjoy how you spend your time.

Chapter **IV**

The Technology

We have already defined computer graphics as images created partially or entirely by computer, and we have noted that the real meaning of the term resides in the context of a particular application. We must, however, make an important distinction between active and passive, or "interactive" and "noninteractive" computer graphics.

Interactive computer graphics requires immediate communication between the machine and the user. The computer must display the user's input in such a manner that the user feels actively in control. Passive, or noninteractive, computer graphics, on the other hand, has no dynamic relationship to the user; the computer displays a finished product that the user cannot modify once he has input the initial graphic data. The mechanical plotting of a drawing, for instance, can occur anytime after the information has been input, and even at different locations.

Interactive computer graphics allows the user to perform many manipulations upon graphic data after it has been input. Whereas the traditional graphic arts limit a designer to a physical product that he can take away at the end of his work, the computer allows a designer an exciting array of options. The computer can store the stages of the creation of an image in memory, so that the designer can go back and modify his plan if he strays in a wrong direction, experiments, or even has a simple accident. Then the computer gives the designer numerous routines that he may utilize to modify, update, or even reformat the graphic data. The computer makes it possible to adjust the size of graphic elements to a different scale, to rotate them in the display, and even to interpolate a three-dimensional image from a two-dimensional model. The two main capacities in which computer graphics differs from the traditional graphic arts are:

1. The computer's ability to store graphic data in memory for updating and manipulation.
2. The computer's ability to manipulate graphic elements within a display by performing the operations of scaling, rotation, and translation.

Computers have been used to draw pictures for over thirty years. They were originally used to display large amounts of numbers and complex data in bar charts, graphs, pie charts, and histograms. The benefit of using the computer to display this kind of information was speed and accuracy. In 1953 the SAGE air traffic control system came into use for detecting and displaying the position of aircraft. Despite SAGE and some other early applications, however, the use of computer graphics was limited during the 1950s. It took extensive computer memory to make an image, and the process was quite slow. Central processing unit (CPU) time was also very expensive; prohibitively so for many possible applications.

In 1962 Ivan E. Sutherland's seminal thesis, "Sketchpad: A Man-Machine Graphical Communications System," brought interactive computer graphics to widespread attention. Sutherland developed this, the first interactive computer graphics system, to fill a Defense Department contract: to build a flight simulator for pilot training that would display exactly the same views a pilot would experience in an actual flying aircraft. His success inspired full-scale computer graphics research and development by organizations with both financial and technical clout: Massachusetts Institute of Technology, Bell Laboratories, General Motors, and Lockheed Aircraft are typical.

Computer graphics was limited in the early 1960s by the state of the hardware. The only display device available was the vector refresh cathode ray tube (CRT). An electron beam drew a picture on the screen as an assembly of straight lines, or vectors, by exciting phosphors on the screen. The picture had to be drawn, or refreshed, at least thirty times per second to give the appearance of a steady image. This made for severe limitations on the number of lines that could be drawn.

The research started to pay off in the 1970s. Improvements were made in both the types of display devices available and the cost of computer time. Microprocessors helped to reduce the bulk that the central processing unit had to process and to focus those tasks. The evolution of the semiconductor chip dramatically reduced the cost of memory. By the early 1980s three kinds of display devices existed that had realistic applications to many situations: the *vector refresh CRT*, the *direct view storage tube CRT*, and the *raster scan CRT*. Raster scan technology opened the door for microcomputer graphics and is bringing computer graphics into the home.

As hardware became more and more sophisticated to meet the need for computerized graphics display, software had to grow too. Software provides the routines with which a designer instructs the computer to perform a specific function and display the result; it provides the interface between the desires of the user and the raw, unfocused potential of the machine.

In the early days of computer graphics, users wrote their own software to realize their own specific needs. Software was created for a particular machine and could not be used on another machine. Similarly, users could not use each other's software without first undergoing an educational process. Moreover, the addition of a device to the system meant that new software had to be developed before the user could utilize the new whole.

By the 1980s the need for and importance of standardized software had become widely recognized. GKS, or Graphical Kernel System, a West Germany–developed programmer interface to graphics, has been largely adopted as an international standard. The main benefit of standardization is portability. Portability means that software developed for one device can be used on another and display exactly the same image. Also, programmers enjoy greater mobility because they can employ their skills on many systems, and employers benefit from not having to train programmers on their particular routine each time they need an addition to their staff.

Humans have been communicating graphically with computers for only a few decades. There is constant demand for both hardware and software that will allow users to do more things more easily. That demand will continue for the foreseeable future. On the bottom line, this reveals the great demand for people who can design better machines, hardware; and for people who make routines that make it easier to communicate with machines, software.

Computer graphics hardware comes in diverse forms. The declining price of computer memory has come to mean that more devices are becoming available to an increasing range of people. Essentially, graphics entails three kinds of devices in addition to the computer itself. *Input devices* digitize a picture or chart, which means that the image is rendered in numbers that describe X, Y, Z coordinates for the computer. *Display devices* both show an image and make it possible for it to be manipulated—the operations of scaling, rotation, and translation, for example. *Output devices* yield a hard copy that can be removed from the computer site for examination or presentation.

Input devices are used to put display data into the computer, or to manipulate data that is already on display. The most common input devices are the tablet, joystick, mouse, light pen, and trackball. The graphic *tablet* is a flat surface under which a grid of wires crosses in the X, Y directions. As a stylus passes over the surface of the tablet, the computer receives X, Y values from each intersection of wires. The stylus can be used both to trace graphics into the computer and to design an original picture. The *joystick* is similar to its counterpart in airplanes. It moves up, down, to the right, and to the left. A cursor on the screen responds to the movement of the joystick in speed as well as direction. The *mouse* is a small box on wheels that is simple to move about by hand. It controls a cursor in a similar manner to the joystick and is used for interacting with a program rather than for inputting data. The *light pen* is a small, hand-held cylinder with a photocell in its tip; software makes the computer sensitive to the photocell when it is switched on. The pen is held directly up to the screen and can both draw and erase lines. The *trackball* is a round ball in a socket that controls a cursor on the screen. The cursor responds to both the speed and direction to which the ball is rotated. Trackballs are widely used to control video game cursors.

An output device renders a copy of the image displayed on the screen on paper or film. Different machines are used for graphs and diagrams than for complexly colored images. The most common graph plotters are drum plotters, flat-bed plotters, and electrostatic plotters. *Drum plotters* are the most widely used and are capable of producing large, complicated colored diagrams. A large "drum" of paper is rotated past several pens, which draw the image by crossing the paper in a direction perpendicular to the paper's unrolling. *Flat-bed plotters* come in different sizes, both small enough to fit on a desktop and up to the size of a large table. Pens are mounted on a gantry, which moves across the flat bed in the X direction. The pens draw by moving up and down the gantry in the Y direction. Flat-bed plotters offer versatility. Any kind of paper can be drawn upon, including transparent overlays. Different numbers and types of pens can be mounted on the gantry to accommodate desired emphasis or style.

Electrostatic plotters show a picture as an assemblage of dots, much as a television picture is rendered. Paper is chemically treated so that the picture can be "charged" onto it by electrodes. The paper then goes through a toner bath where the charged dots pick up black coloring. The electrostatic plotter is useful for its ability to plot rapidly. It does not offer high-quality resolution and is not suited for precise plans or drawings.

Several devices are used to output color copy. These include camera systems, matrix printers, ink-jet plotters, and film recorders. The easiest and least expensive way to obtain a color copy is to hold a camera up to the display and take a picture, and this is often done. High-quality cameras, when carefully used, can produce a reasonable facsimile. However, the curvature of the screen generally makes for some distortion around the edges of the picture, and color does not always translate precisely between the mediums. For that reason, video signal camera systems were developed. These systems connect directly to the display signal and can actually output higher-quality images than the display itself. This requires very intricate equipment and considerable expense.

Matrix printers utilize several color ribbons to deposit an image, usually yellow, magenta, and cyan. Paper passes through the printer for one color, then is wound back and sent through again for the next. The color is deposited as a matrix of dots. The dots can be deposited in varied combinations and densities so that a range of color is available. The benefit of the matrix printer is that it is fast and relatively inexpensive, but it does not yield a smoothly finished product.

Ink-jet plotters shoot a very fine spray of ink onto paper from three colored jets, yellow, magenta, and cyan. Ink-jet plotters can produce high-quality shading quickly, since only one pass of the paper is required. They are becoming increasingly popular for this reason.

Display devices show the graphic that is being constructed or inspected on the screen. They are traditionally associated with two types of cathode ray tubes: random scan and raster scan. Random scans trace out a programmed line, and raster scans illuminate groups of dots like a television picture.

Direct-view storage tubes were developed to examine images that do not require much changing, such as architectural plans and circuit diagrams. They produce a steady, flicker-free image because the picture is drawn semipermanently onto the screen itself. The screen is coated with long-persistence phosphors, which glow as they are excited by an electron gun that "writes" the image on the screen. The direct-view storage tube yields a good image and is not particularly expensive, but it does have limitations. Part of the picture cannot be changed or updated, the picture does not offer contrast in brightness, and there is no color capacity.

Vector refresh displays utilize short-persistence phosphors and permit interaction and some animation. The picture must be redrawn or refreshed repeatedly, usually between thirty and fifty times a second. Because of this they tend to be quite expensive, and the picture flickers when it becomes complex. Vector refresh displays can be interacted with—usually with a light pen—and offer high resolution with contrast. Some color vector refresh displays are available, usually incorporated into expensive computer generation systems for a specific task that requires high quality. The performance of these systems is limited because they offer few colors, have low brightness, and flicker if the display becomes too complex.

Until the late 1960s the storage tube and vector refresh displays were the only systems available. Both were expensive, and neither was extensively employed. Attention began to center on a way to utilize television technology to produce a display, and the *raster scan* was the result. Like a television screen, the display screen of a raster device is divided into a matrix or "raster" of dots. A common number is 512 x 512, and the total number of dots is called the resolution of the screen. Screens with much greater resolution are presently under development. Each dot is called a picture element, or *pixel*. The computer memorizes information for every pixel location. Three color electron guns—red, blue, and green—shoot beams at a metal masking device, which controls the areas of phosphors on the screen to be excited. Raster scans yield a bright, interactively controllable image in which many colors can be generated. The drawbacks of rasters scans are that they require a great deal of computer memory and have limited resolution. Straight diagonal lines can show a slight "staircasing" effect, as lines are connected from dot to dot and not actually drawn. Raster scans offer flicker-free complex images and generate color very quickly. They are compatible with television technology; TV pictures can be frozen and have raster graphics added. With the ability to shade colors for texture and illumination, raster scans offer the closest approximation of reality.

Direct-view storage tube and vector refresh displays are best when a high-resolution black-and-white line drawing is desired. They are used most widely for highly technical applications, such as engineering and architecture. Raster scans were developed for a broader spectrum of applications and are very adaptable. They are widely used for simulation animation and design applications. Raster scans are more economical, and are becoming increasingly popular.

Chapter **V**

The Microcomputer and the Future

The future of computer graphics will be played out largely on microcomputers. Rapid advances in technology are making it possible for more and more graphics functions to be done on the smaller, more portable, less expensive machine. The microcomputer is presently used most widely in business for the generation of charts and graphs for presentation and decision support, and for data management. Several manufacturers have added paint systems to their microcomputers, usually through a tablet and stylus configuration, and these can produce color images on a color monitor or from a color printer.

Significantly, small vendors of hardware and services are tending to soup up IBM PCs (PC, XT, AT) with extra memory, sharper graphics, and imaginative software to produce highly competent graphics workstations for both art and CAD applications. These systems still cost far more than a basic microcomputer alone, but with costs ranging between $7,000 and $35,000 they are far more affordable than top-end mini and mainframe systems, which can run over $100,000. The IBM PC is preferred over other PCs because of IBM's tendency to set the standards that the computer industry follows, and because of a widely held assumption that IBM will soon come out with its own graphics workstations in the $10,000 to $20,000 range.

It can only be expected that this trend toward microcomputer enhancement will continue until microcomputers can perform all but the most sophisticated tasks that the larger mini and mainframe computers perform today. As the ability to perform graphics functions becomes decentralized and disseminated on a wide scale, opportunities for entrepreneurs starting up with a small investment—and really all kinds of artists and designers who want to produce sophisticated finished work without becoming associated with a major corporation—will not only grow but broaden in scope.

Already there is burgeoning growth in computer-aided design on the microcomputer, which differs from full-blown CAD-/CAM only in scale. The computer enhances the design process in the creation of virtually any desired object. Current applications include the design of textiles, cards, fabrics, jewelry, and original fonts.

The microcomputer is well suited and widely employed for educational purposes. Graphics have several valuable applications in computer-aided learning (CAL), and with imagination these can extend limitlessly. Graphics are already used in the education of very young children who, because of their lack of mathematical and verbal sophistication, would otherwise have little use for a computer. Images prompt them to respond to the computer and bring them into the learning process itself in an engaging manner: for pushing the right button they are rewarded with the desired image on the screen. Not only will computerphobia be a meaningless word to students who are introduced early to the computer, but also their ability to assimilate knowledge will be enhanced. They will visualize physical aspects of the world such as shape, size, and scale long before they learn geometry. As they develop, mathematical models will have visual analogs, rather than just existing as long rows of alphanumerics.

On a more sophisticated level, computer graphics can give breathtaking views of the physical sciences. The computer can image anything that can be described mathematically, regardless of whether the description is theoretical. From the creation of the universe in the big bang, to the molecular structure of an atom, to the building of the pyramids stone by stone, students can view processes actually occurring. In one of several areas where the computer is effective for research as well as teaching, biochemists use computer simulations to investigate the molecular structure of viruses.

Beyond helping to teach technical and practical skills, CAL systems have been used to help handicapped people who need extra instruction or who cannot reach the classroom. The microcomputer offers many benefits for home study; if it is connected to another computer at a school, a dynamic learning environment exists. One special graphic program that has been designed helps people with hearing defects to master lipreading. The mouth position for each phonetic sound can be displayed, and the student follows the computer sound by sound until he becomes fast enough to follow entire sentences.

The microcomputer has been used in education only for a short time, and its possible beneficial uses have only begun to be explored. Graphics will play a leading role with the microcomputer in CAL by helping to make information more easily understood, more visually impactful, and more fun to interact with. Already, there are graphics packages on microcomputers for learning to type—traditionally a tedious task—that use the properly struck key to shoot down space invader–type objects. After becoming skilled at this engaging video game, a person finds himself able to type.

CAL should especially benefit the gifted child. With his computer, he will be able to play out scenarios as sophisticated as his imagination, rather than being tied to the plodding pace of "average" for which most textbooks are written. As the microcomputer becomes widely available in the early grades and preschool, society may discover more and more child prodigies whose years of play have culminated in designs with fresh, original points of view.

In business, microcomputers are being linked together in groups to form local area networks (LANs). LANs are groups of microcomputers linked together into a synergistic whole that can command greater total processing power than a minicomputer. (These networks are "local" because the computers are physically connected by hardware such as wire or coaxial cable.) Each individual computer can share files from any other computer in the network and can use remote resources like a high quality plotter, just as if it were directly linked. Total shipments of microcomputer LANs are expected to double annually over the next five years; 20 to 30 percent of all microcomputers are expected to be connected in LANs by the end of that time.

One of the implications of the growth of LANs in the office is that there will be less need for hard copy—paper. Where in the past displays were created on one computer, printed on paper, and then distributed by hand, managers and data processors can be able to view information directly and immediately on their own screen. In the future, more and more display information, both graphic and alphanumeric, will remain in the video environment. The computer can efficiently store (file), display, and distribute information; there will be less and less need for the computer to provide hard copy as users become accustomed to operating through their own monitors. LANs are already being extended into wide-area networks (WANs), and special "gateways" that can link geographically remote clusters of LANs are being developed.

In the office of the future, providers of goods and services and their clients will simultaneously view identical displays to evaluate performance and develop strategy. Graphics will play an increasingly important role as executives view summary data while on conference calls and play out "what if" scenarios on their individual displays. Where today's executive spends much of his time sitting at his desk and struggling with the paper monster, the executive of the future will likely sit—without a desk—in front of a wall-sized display, testing out his hypotheses with an interactive device such as a joystick.

In science and engineering, computer graphics will provide dramatic increases in productivity. Databases shared through LANs will connect all of a corporation's technical people. With improved three-dimensional modeling, the prototype stage of product development will be entirely eliminated. Products will be created, designed, tested, and sent for manufacturing right on the screen. Freed from the pressure of many intermediate steps in the production process, technical designers will be able to achieve more creativity than ever before. The increased number of possibilities that the computer allows the designer to explore will be reflected in innovations in the architectural landscape surrounding us.

Computer graphics will literally revolutionize contemporary and traditional notions of entertainment. Today's interactive video game will be like a prehistoric forebear to full-scale computer simulation. Without leaving their living room, people will actually experience flying a jet plane or climbing Mount Everest.

Virtually the whole world will have a good idea of what it is like to fly in a space shuttle and will visit the rings of Saturn via satellite. Wall-size display devices will make it possible to create different ambient environments to suit different moods. People may choose to be surrounded by gently whispering surf while they write letters, or by an explosive rock concert while aerobicising (exercising on a stationary bicycle will come close to participating in the Tour de France).

In art, canvas will likely give way to video as more and more art is created for and viewed on VDTs. Animations will become increasingly complex and realistic. As the performance of the human body can be described more accurately, ballets will be choreographed and Super Bowls planned on computers. The addition of computerized special effects and animation capability to video cassettes will make possible home movies with more sparkle than "Dallas" or "Dynasty."

Chapter VI

Computer Graphics and Your Health

Are video display terminals (VDTs) safe? The jury is still out on that question. Cathode ray tubes (CRTs), which constitute the glowing screen within the VDT, do emit some radiation. Because of this, they have been accused of generating vision problems, aggravating cardiac conditions, and causing pregnant women who have been exposed to the screen to miscarry or bear deformed infants. Workers' organizations such as the Service Employees International Union (SEIU) and 9to5, the Association of Working Women are demanding more protection. They cite statistics about "clusters" of incidents among VDT workers and point to the CRT as the cause. On the other side, manufacturers, represented by the Computer and Business Equipment Manufacturers Association (CBEMA), claim that CRTs do not emit enough radioactivity to be harmful. Their analysis of the statistics finds no "clusters" and even points to the safety of CRT work because of the great numbers of VDT workers who have had no problems.

At present, eighteen state legislatures either have bills before them to regulate the conditions of VDT work or have initiated studies to decide whether legislation should be considered. The SEIU and 9to5 are lobbying for still more legislation in more states. Within their own organizations, some states and Canadian provinces have devised guidelines to restrict VDT work and allow pregnant women to be excused from it completely.

The workers' organizations insist that there is a clear and present danger and charge that workers are being used like laboratory animals while substantive data is collected. They point to "clusters" of incidents in which VDT workers suffer abnormally high rates of problems—higher than non-VDT workers who perform similar tasks. Danger to pregnant women has been the most volatile, most widely publicized issue. Higher incidence of cardiac problems has also been charged. Less severe problems such as eyestrain and backache are the most widely experienced.

So far, manufacturers have been able to come up with good answers to most of the charges. Because of the negative image resulting from the somewhat hysterical publicity that blames the CRT for incidents, CBEMA has moved to inform the public and the media. They insist that CRTs emit only a negligible amount of radiation. Radiation occurs in the natural environment continually; it is emitted by our own bodies and by scores of inanimate objects. Manufacturers maintain that CRTs radiate at such low levels that their emissions cannot be distinguished from other background radiation.

Manufacturers and health regulatory agencies have conducted in-depth investigations of many of the "clusters" of problems suffered by pregnant women. Manufacturers argue that the numbers involved are not statistically significant, but of more importance is the fact that no investigation has charged the CRT with responsibility. Workers' organizations argue that manufacturers approach the matter with protection of their own vested interests in mind, yet health and regulatory officials have failed so far to implicate the CRT.

Perhaps aggravating the controversy is the fact that many people don't fully realize how great the hazards involved in childbearing. A significant percentage of conceptions result in miscarriage, and when successful pregnancies that yield infants with birth defects are factored in, the percentage increases. Investigations of CRT-related pregnancy incidents have often revealed hereditary predisposition to problems or poor pregnancy care. Family history and prenatal care have been proven to affect delivery; the CRT has not.

The American Academy of Ophthalmology has concluded that VDTs are safe for normal use and are not hazardous to vision. Eyestrain, however, remains one of the most common complaints among VDT operators. Since the CRT screen is coated with glass, considerable glare results if there is bright lighting in the work area. Most offices were not designed for use of VDTs, and many still do not recognize the need for low light levels. Some operators still require corrective lenses to help them focus on the screen.

Several simple things can be done to help avoid eyestrain. The first is to be aware of lighting levels and make sure there is good contrast and no glare. Next, operators should make a point of frequently looking away from the screen and focusing on a distant object. This change in focus is very refreshing to the eyes. Last, workers should remember to blink. When workers get involved with the VDT, they tend to blink less often and their eyes become dry and irritated. Since focusing on a VDT is different from focusing on a piece of paper, workers who experience problems should not hesitate to consult an ophthalmologist, even if they have previously been trouble-free.

Backache problems have a cause in common with eyestrain: office design. Operators generally have to sit quite close to the VDT, and in offices that are not designed for the purpose, uncomfortable working positions have often resulted. Workers should attempt to accommodate their own personal style in their work arrangements. Lounging back in a springy chair is just as acceptable as sitting up in a straight-backed chair, provided comfort is achieved. Physical discomfort tends to aggravate other problems, particularly irritation and stress. Many workers prefer the detached keyboard, which they can adjust to their individual way of sitting.

Studies have been conducted that show a higher level of complaints about angina and chest pains among VDT workers than among non-VDT workers performing similar tasks. Again, however, the numbers involved in the sample and the percentage of deviation are both too small to support conclusions. Since stress is a major contributor to heart problems and VDT work is inherently more stressful than non-VDT work, it has been observed that stress, rather than CRT emissions, may be responsible for the alleged aggravation of heart problems. VDT work generally entails more time pressure in the production of work and more rapid accountability for the quality of the work that is done. Any large company or organization wants to see worker efficiency justifying the cost of computer time and hardware. When workers have to endure both poor physical comfort and a bad visual environment, the effects of marginal stress are likely to be intensified.

Stress is present in many computer graphics applications areas. As the computer helps make the production of images more efficient, demands for even greater speed arise from a population that still regards computers as "magic machines" capable of instantaneous creation. The fact that expensive computer systems can be utilized around the clock may prompt firms to adopt multiple-shift workdays to maximize the return on their investment. This forces designers and artists in areas that have not traditionally faced strict deadlines to deal with daily, unremitting time pressure. Someone is waiting for their chair when their eight hours are up, even though they still need one more to finish. Junior people especially face having to switch abruptly from a day shift to a night shift, or else possibly lose their job.

Stress has traditionally been a part of a successful career, and there are no indications that it will cease to be so. But as regards the potential hazards of the VDT itself, research into both the effects on VDT users and the mechanism of the CRT itself promises to yield substantive results within the next decade. The National Institute for Occupational Safety and Health (NIOSH) is presently initiating major research on the effects of the VDT on pregnant women. Of the scale of studies that documented the dangers of smoking and asbestos, the study is to involve 3,000 women of childbearing age and follow them for three years.

When all the evidence is weighed, the final word on VDT use and health is: Caution. Although none of the charges against the CRT have been substantiated and many singular incidents have been satisfactorily explained, the fact that enough incidents have been reported to raise safety questions demands prudence. VDT users should be particularly sensitive to the overall comfort of their working environment, to avoid aggravating any occupational stress with unnecessary problems such as eyestrain and backache. Pregnant women should exercise particular caution and consult with their obstetrician.

Part 2
Applications

Introduction

This section describes some of the applications of computer graphics in the real world. While the sample here is necessarily finite, it should give some indication of the virtually unlimited range of possible applications.

Applications areas are broken down into three rough divisions: Art/Animation, CAD/CAM, and Business. A graph detailing the projected growth for that sector of the industry precedes each division.* For Art/Animation and CAD/CAM, a

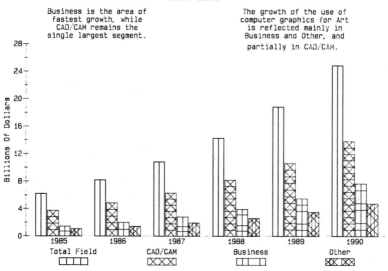

COMPUTER GRAPHICS GROWTH BY SEGMENT
1985-1990

Business is the area of fastest growth, while CAD/CAM remains the single largest segment.

The growth of the use of computer graphics for Art is reflected mainly in Business and Other, and partially in CAD/CAM.

*Outlook figures are based on projected growth of sales of hardware and software in the commercial/industrial sector.

job ladder describing job progression and salary is given for several occupations. Since Business is such a broad area, a job ladder has not been included.

Studies have not shown that computer graphics practitioners make more than the standard salary for each area. In the future, rather than affecting salary levels within an occupation, computer graphics will simply be a part of that occupation. There has, however, been talk among insiders in the CAD/CAM sector of companies pirating top people from other companies. If that is the case, there is a premium on good people with immediately applicable system experience: a company has to offer more money to induce someone to leave his present position.

Computer graphics tends to affect opportunity in general, rather than salary specifically. A person with computer graphics knowledge has the advantage of an extra qualification at the entry level. Farther along the career path, he will be able to take advantage of this knowledge to enhance his job performance and career progression. In the more technical applications areas such as engineering, the person with computer graphics knowledge today will not have to fear the wave of computer graphics specialists that will emerge from the schools tomorrow.

Computer graphics practitioners in every applications area report that their jobs are stressful. Although stress seems to accompany almost any high-salaried position, in some cases the computer may add extra pressure by holding its user to a closely monitored standard of accountability. In CAD applications, for example, as a rough rule of thumb the productivity per worker at a dedicated graphics workstation averages between $50,000 and $100,000 a year. Workers who fall below this range will experience extra stress, and employers will continually try to coax more productivity out of workers until they feel a maximum has been achieved. In all applications the computer speeds the production of images. Workers may have to contend with time pressure that doesn't understand that humans work differently from computers.

The interviews in Part 3, Career Profiles, give a more in-depth perspective on four applications areas.

Chapter VII

Art and Animation

ART

The use of computer graphics for art applications is projected to increase dramatically over the next five years. While the estimated rate of growth for art is 35 percent annually, the area may develop even faster as it receives additional stimulus from the business sector.

Four representative areas that computer graphics will affect in the near future have been chosen for job ladder descriptions: publishing, advertising, design, and television (video).

The ladder is broken down into four levels that reflect a common progression from the entry-level junior artist to the experienced senior artist who assumes creative responsibility for both large and small projects. Creative director has been included for advertising as the next career progression from senior art director. Creative directors are responsible for the entire creative development of an advertisement or commercial, rather than just the art area. Artists do move into directing in video and film, but that is more of a career change than a natural development.

While the single most important element an artist must display to get work is a strong portfolio, a bachelor's degree is generally advisable. Artists who work in a business environment are expected to communicate effectively and to take responsibility for some degree of routine administration.

To progress to the higher salary levels, an artist must produce quality work, usually under restrictive time pressure. He should also possess some business sense; understanding the degree to which his talent is in demand will help him determine how large a salary he can command or whether he can attract business on his own. Whereas a businessman seeks to progress through relatively standard levels, a successful artist needs to cultivate his own distinctive style.

PROJECTED GROWTH FOR ART/ANIMATION
1985-1990 ·
In Billions Of Dollars

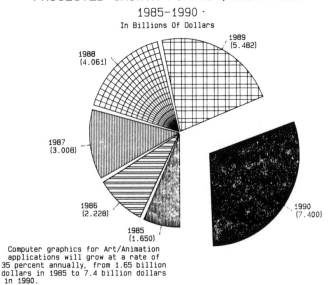

1989
(5.482)

1988
(4.061)

1987
(3.008)

1986
(2.228)

1985
(1.650)

1990
(7.400)

Computer graphics for Art/Animation applications will grow at a rate of 35 percent annually, from 1.65 billion dollars in 1985 to 7.4 billion dollars in 1990.

CAREER LADDER—ART AND ANIMATION

Publishing/Advertising		Design Firm		Television (Video)	
Art Director's Assistant	$12–15K	Assistant Designer	$15K	Production Assistant	$25K
Junior Art Director	20–25K	Junior Designer	25K	Designer/Illustrator	35–40K
Art Director	35–45K	Designer	35K	Senior Designer	45–55K
Senior Art Director	50–60K	Senior Designer	40–50K	(Director/Producer?)	
Creative Director	75–100+K				

Vice President	50K+
Senior Vice President	60K+
Executive Vice President	100K+
President	100K+

In each of these categories it is possible to move up into management, with titles like vice president, senior vice president, and president coming next. To go beyond approximately the 50k level, many artists branch off into their own business. This usually means becoming a partner in an advertising agency, a production company, or a design firm. Many artists also develop a free-lance business, usually by taking on a few clients while they keep their full-time job, and eventually getting enough clients to become self-employed. Free-lance opportunities will increase for computer graphic artists as the price of hardware comes down and as microcomputers become more sophisticated, permitting the production of high-quality work in the home.

Fine art is presently created on computers, and in the future computer art may well come to represent an entire discipline in itself. However, the feast or famine (mostly famine) income levels traditionally associated with fine art will probably prevail for computer art as well.

Perhaps the fastest-growing area of computer graphics is commercial graphic design. Not only can the computer help the graphic artist develop more pictures in less time, but it also makes available effects that would be extremely difficult and expensive to achieve in any other way. Human creativity and judgment still retain primary importance, because the computer also makes it easier to create pictures and graphs that communicate poorly or are hard on the eye. The task of the graphic artist—producing slides, transparencies, pictures for books and magazines, posters for billboards and exhibitions, and stills for television and film—remains to present material in a visually engaging manner. The computer is a sophisticated tool, but still no more than a tool.

An examination of Quantel's digital Paint Box System illustrates some of the advantages the computer can give to the graphic artist. This system is intended to provide the artist with the colors, brushes, scissors, glue, rulers, and typefaces that he would normally have available. The first problem a system designed for graphic artists must solve is how the artist will input data in a natural way and then react to and interact with the picture he has created. Systems have been developed in which images can be drawn directly on touch-sensitive screens or with a mouse or joystick controlling the pen (cursor) position on the display. The method that has come to be preferred is the use of a digitizer, or "touch tablet" and a stylus. The Quantel Paint Box employs this method, with an extremely sensitive stylus. It answers to the pressure of the hand, making the process of drawing and painting feel more natural. It also is versatile, giving the artist the immediate option of switching among five modes:

1. Paint: Used for basic drawing and resembles regular oils in appearance. The stylus deposits the color thinly on the

screen when light pressure is applied and thickly when the pressure is heavy.

2. Wash: Used to create an effect similar to watercolors. The screen can be covered in color, but underlying detail will not be lost.
3. Shade: Used for tinting and shading areas. As opposed to wash, it gives complete control of the tonal range.
4. Chalk: Gives a gritty texture and is useful for suggesting depth and solidity. The result is reminiscent of crayon or chalk.
5. Air brush: Used to indicate softness and changes in texture. The computer uses a "spray" of fine dots to achieve the same effect as a spray of paint.

The artist also has the option of selecting from stylus sizes that correspond to the range between fine tip and wide brush. The Paint Box offers further facilities that enable the artist to go beyond what he could create by traditional means. He can magnify a particular section of an image to enhance detail and use the electronic equivalent of scissors and glue to cut, resize, fuse, rotate, and move pictures or parts of pictures anywhere on the screen. In addition, the Paint Box can accept live video input. A television picture can be frozen on the screen and then treated like any other picture. It can be retouched, have additional graphics inserted, and have text incorporated.

A recent application of the Paint Box is the generation of professional fonts. Traditional graphic artists have been limited to a fixed number of typefaces, with little control over letter spacing and positioning. With the Paint Box fonts can be selected, altered to any size or color, and combined with special effects to give many different images, for instance, a solid, 3D look.

ANIMATION

Animation is one of the most involved and rewarding applications for the graphic artist. In television commercials and in major movies, computer animation is providing the new, high-profile images that compel the viewer's attention. The computer can be used for both the simpler, two-dimensional animation and full-scale three-dimensional computer imaging. The traditional method of producing a Walt Disney–type cartoon has always been labor-intensive and repetitive. After a story line and sound track are agreed upon, the main animators draw the most important, or "key," frames that show action. The frames in between are drawn by assistants. All the drawings are then transferred to celluloid and colored by hand.

The computer can streamline the animation in several ways. It can color in all frames. Once the color values have been input, the machine is ideal for this repetitive task. It can actually draw transitional frames. Called "key frame in betweening," this has achieved great popularity. Once the key frames are programmed in, the computer interpolates the simple action indicated. The computer can perform another manipulation to produce animation that does not correspond to traditional methods. Since the computer has values for the colors it displays in the animated pictures, it can indicate motion simply by switching colors on and off. For instance, it could show the mercury in a thermometer falling by filling in the red with the background color. The creative artist can use color table animation to achieve a wide variety of effects.

There has been increasing demand from the television and film industries for striking three-dimensional images. The computer can be programmed to describe objects as three-dimensional outlines, which are then colored in to produce the desired effect. To aid the animator in creating unusual perspectives, many computer film companies have systems that encompass almost all of the properties of a motion picture camera. The artist should feel comfortable as he interacts with zooms, twists, and other changes in perspective.

Beyond three-dimensional outline animation, in which the computer and the animator share tasks, is full-scale computer imaging. The most recent surface modeling techniques, combined with new ways of generating reflections, shadows, and textures, have made the computer a powerful tool for comprehensive animation. Many companies have now developed computer imaging services. Several collaborated on the Disney film *Tron*, for instance, a feature-length animated movie generated entirely by computer. With its youth, computer imaging carries a high price tag. Models for each desired image must be described mathematically and fed into a powerful computer with a great deal of memory. The process requires creative ingenuity, intensive labor, and a very expensive computer. The benefits of computer imaging are so great, however, that the prognosis for its future development is healthy indeed.

A major advantage of computer imaging over traditional animation is its flexibility in yielding changes of perspective and scale. Environments are displayed with a high degree of detail. Viewpoints can be changed, objects like spaceships can be moved about within the display, and changes in light like the growth of shadows can occur continually.

Computer imaging is especially useful in giving life to objects and events that can be defined mathematically. Processes and objects that would be difficult to illustrate traditionally—many even to conceptualize—can be brought to life by the computer. From the microscopic to the astronomical, events that are dictated by the laws of physics can be shown actually unfolding. This application is especially valuable when applied to research and education.

COMPUTER IMAGE GENERATION
AND SIMULATION

Simulation of highly complicated or technical tasks is valuable for training people in a safe, easily monitored environment. Simulation also provides opportunity in a number of research areas. Traditionally, providing simulations has been extremely expensive, and many areas of the real world have defied imitation. Computer image generation enjoys increasing use and popularity for two reasons. The first is cost; although the computer system necessary for high-quality simulation is quite expensive, it still costs less than real-world alternatives; for instance, in training fighter pilots the computer simulation can reduce the number of training planes necessary. Second, the computer can model processes and products and give views that could not be obtained otherwise. Computer image generation is being used in such industries as engineering, medicine, chemistry, and oil drilling. It is used to train and test pilots and navigators for both civil and military aircraft and ships.

Computer image generation attempts to simulate part of the real world in a fashion as consistent with visual reality as possible and to give interactive control to the operator. In some situations the operator can realize views and perform manipulations that would not otherwise be possible. Biologists can rotate strings of molecules for inspection, paring away and then reassembling layers as they wish. Surgeons examine simulations of the growth of cancer, contrasting and extrapolating upon data as they search for the key to a cure. Perhaps the most exciting use of computer image generation is in the simulation of dynamic environments for ship and aircraft operators.

Simulators for ships have been in use for over a decade. Pilots and navigators can be exposed to numerous situations, both routine and extremely rare. They perceive the action that is taking place in real time, and their manipulation of the controls produces a response in the situation precisely as it would in the real world. External conditions change to their view, including weather fronts moving in, other ships participating in the same locale, and light changes indicating movement from day into night or vice versa.

Ship simulators offer a number of beneficial uses. Pilot and navigator candidates can be given their training and quickly evaluated for potential. Reactions can be tested and rehearsed for dangerous situations involving mechanical failure, inclement weather, other ships, or any combination of the three. Operations such as complicated docking procedures or navigating in problem waters can be rehearsed with the actual docks or waters simulated. When personnel are transferred to a different type of ship, they can be quickly familiarized with its operation. The next step after simulating an existing ship is to simulate a ship that is still in the planning stages. Ship designs are simulated for research purposes and tested under various conditions. Ports, approaches, and traffic-control systems can be evaluated for different combinations of types and numbers of ships under various weather conditions.

The reality provided by ship simulators is such that the operator becomes completely involved in his situation, realizing the significance of his actions and the importance of his responsibility. A real bridge analog is constructed as the site for the exercise; when the operator transfers to an actual ship there is no loss of familiarity. A special benefit of simulation is that an instructor can monitor the operator's progress and pose problems from the outside, thus focusing real-life experience through computer technology for the most effective training.

Computer-controlled flight simulators were first used in the 1960s and are widely employed for military planes, large commercial planes, and some helicopters. In the simulations the control cabin is copied down to the merest detail. The pilot sees a complete range of view out of his windows, as if he were actually airborne. This effect comes from both high-quality computer-generated displays behind each window and a motion control unit that tilts the cockpit to the angle corresponding to the craft's attitude in actual flight.

Simulators are even more valuable for planes than for ships because of the greater speed at which situations develop in the air and the lethal consequence of mishap. Pilots are exposed to and trained for situations they will almost certainly encounter, such as inclement weather and difficult landings—night landing on an aircraft carrier, for example. But they also face potential situations that would be impossible to experience in a real-life mock-up. Among these are collision with another plane, various mechanical failures, and complete combat situations. An instructor takes the pilot through step by step, so he becomes experienced before he encounters potentially life-endangering situations.

Simulation through computer image generation offers opportunity for research and training at a lower cost than is possible in many real-life situations. The computer makes it possible to experience situations that would be prohibitively dangerous otherwise, and it permits viewing of objects and processes from any desired vantagepoint.

Chapter **VIII**

CAD/CAM

CAD/CAM will comprise the single largest computer graphics segment through 1990. While CAD/CAM will generate significant new employment opportunities, it will also have dramatic effect on traditional technical occupations in which professionals routinely need to become proficient on a system.

Three representative areas in which CAD/CAM will play a large role in the future have been chosen for job ladder description: architecture, engineering, and chemistry.

The ladder is broken down into eight levels, in a format sim-

GV21-0100 Design Model IBM 5080 Graphics Subsystem

ilar to that of the U.S. Bureau of Labor Statistics. Job titles are given for architecture, as an architect generally progresses through titled levels. Although the titles "engineer" and "chemist" tend to be inclusive, the job levels for chemistry and engineering compare to those for architecture in seniority, ability, and responsibility, if not in title. In general, the levels reflect experience, the difficulty of required tasks, and the amount of managerial supervision performed.

Second only to teaching as the largest profession in the U.S., engineering covers too wide a range to be broken down in detail. More than twenty-five specialties are recognized by professional engineering societies, and each has multiple subdivisions. The most common are aerospace, agricultural, biomedical, chemical, civil, electrical/electronic, mechanical, metallurgical/materials, mining, nuclear, and petroleum.

Engineers are judged largely on the results of what they produce. To move beyond the lower middle salary level, an engineer must exhibit the ability to be innovative and to solve problems.

Engineers with a doctorate tend to fare significantly better in salary, while engineers with a master's degree fare only slightly better than those with a bachelor's degree. In most cases, a bachelor's degree is necessary to enter the field.

Chemists work in a wide range of private industry, not just in university laboratories. They are needed in the production of all manner of products, from packaged foods to synthetic fabrics. The main branches of chemistry are analytical, organic, inorganic, and physical.

An advanced degree is usually necessary for a chemist to progress beyond the level of technician. Like engineers, chemists have to produce to excel. To reach the higher salary levels, a chemist must go beyond the routine administration of tests and contribute insight.

ARCHITECTURE

Computer graphics will quite literally add another dimension to architectural design. The architect has always been tied to two-dimensional representations to conceive and develop an idea and then present it to a client. The production of the small-

PROJECTED GROWTH FOR CAD/CAM
1985-1990

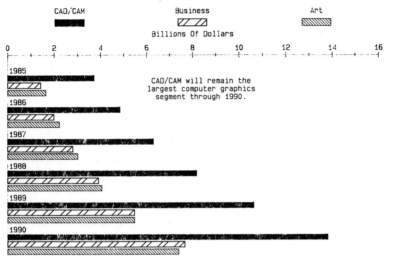

CAD/CAM

Business

Art

Billions Of Dollars

CAD/CAM will remain the
largest computer graphics
segment through 1990.

1985

1986

1987

1988

1989

1990

CAREER LADDER—CAD/CAM

ARCHITECTURE			CHEMISTRY		ENGINEERING	
Level		Salary	Level	Salary	Level	Salary
I	Junior Designer/Draftsman	$19,250	I	$19,500	I	$23,500
II	Designer Draftsman	$20,500	II	$23,000	II	$26,000
III	Senior Draftsman/Designer	$24,000	III	$27,500	III	$30,000
IV	Job/Project Captain	$27,000	IV	$34,000	IV	$34,000
V	Senior Job/Project Captain	$28,500	V	$40,000	V	$40,500
VI	Project Manager/Project Architect	$32,000	VI	$45,000	VI	$46,000
VII	Senior Project Mgr/Administrator	$36,000	VII	$52,000	VII	$53,500
VIII	Principal Designer	$43,000	VIII	—	VIII	$62,000

Owner/Partner $100,000+ Top-Echelon Executive

The most successful architects go on to become partners in prestigious firms or to found their own
firms. Principals in architectural firms can earn $150K+.

The top end for engineering traditionally does not extend as far as that for architecture; however,
engineers often become principals in their own contracting or consulting firms, where they can enjoy
substantial incomes. Engineering also can open the door to top-echelon management. Engineers are
prominent in the management of the auto industry, for example, where top executives regularly make
$100K+.

While chemistry tends not to be associated with business, those chemists who reach the highest levels
in industry can gain entrée into top management. Consulting also can be lucrative for sought-after
chemists.

scale model can come only after the blueprinting is completed. With computer graphics, the architect can not only expedite the creation and display of blueprints but also can display complete three-dimensional models and even conduct complex performance analyses—all before the first shovel of earth has been turned.

The most common use of computer graphics in architecture is in drafting. Firms produce great quantities of design plans, ranging from simple dimension indicators to complex series of overlays showing details including the location of major pieces of furniture. Using the computer, the architect can perform many manipulations as soon as the data has been input. He can have any section of the plan rotated, scaled, copied, moved, deleted, or filled in. He can focus on any part of the plan to make detailed adjustments. This flexibility not only allows for more functional experimentation and esthetic expression by the individual architect, but also permits greater communication on specifics among several architects, engineers, interior decorators, and clients.

Once the three-dimensional X,Y,Z coordinates have been specified, the computer can render a three-dimensional perspective drawing from any viewpoint the architect wishes. Models can be viewed in relationship to the building site from every direction. With the latest software, models can now be shaded in. Architects can assess the impact of a building at different times of day and different seasons of the year. When the architectural firm is also responsible for elements of interior design, three-dimensional model shading can be utilized to create many arrangements of rooms, from door and window sites to coloring and lighting arrangements. At this stage, the client can view the graphics and exercise his own choice of arrangement.

Although esthetic positioning is always important—particularly in today's vertically escalating urban environment—a building is designed to fulfill certain functions. The computer can analyze vast amounts of numbers describing how a building will actually perform and render the data in graphs, charts, and tables. Performance analysis attempts to cover all the variables from maximum space utilization to the effect of climate, from the accessibility of necessary heavy equipment to the cost of all materials. The computer makes data for both projected and occurring performance analysis readily accessible.

Architects and engineers must analyze how the geometrical configuration they desire in a structure will perform under stress. The computer can break down complex objects and structures into simple parts and then test each part and specify its contribution to the total system. To analyze the tremendous mass of geometrical, topological, and climatic information, the architect and engineer can view color-coded representations of the stress parameters and accurately anticipate structural behavior.

It should be noted that while many architectural firms are employing computer graphics, many still rely on traditional methods. This is partly because developing a computer system requires an expensive commitment, and partly because some architects resist what they see as the interference of the machine in the creative process. As more architectural projects are completed with the assistance of the computer, professionals will realize that computer graphics is only a tool. While it is the most modern tool and offers comprehensive benefits, it possesses no more inherent creativity than dividers, compass, or T square.

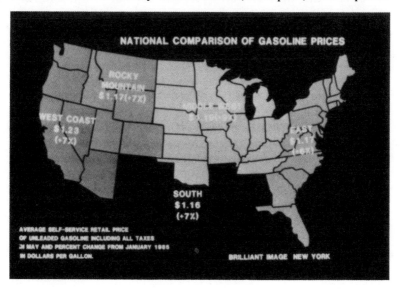

The computer is useful for presenting geographical data.

Mapping

The computer is useful for presenting geographical data about land use, taxation, distribution of services, climate, demography, topography, or anything for which statistics are available. It can make changes and update data far more rapidly than an artist could by hand. In some situations, it provides special benefits because it can offer different views. When the topology of an area is being analyzed, for instance, the computer can display different angles of view until the most informative one is found.

ENGINEERING

Computer-aided design and manufacturing (CAD/CAM) systems are having a strong impact on a wide spectrum of engineering applications. Engineers apply basically the same computer graphics functions as do architects. CAD/CAM systems help them to design and test mechanical and electrical structures and to project and account for costs accurately. The computer helps to streamline the design and manufacture of virtually any element, from a cog in a wheel to a whole factory.

Perhaps the most dramatic changes are occurring in the area of structural analysis and design. Computerized routines have made finite-element methods of stress analysis available for evaluating building structures in architecture, for engineering vehicle dynamics in the aerospace and automotive fields, and in the production of mechanical parts.

In the finite-element method, simply shaped elements interconnect to form a whole complex object. Structural equations specify the contribution of each element to the whole, so that a combination of the individual elements indicates how the structure as a whole will perform. An important benefit of computerized stress analysis is creativity: Engineers can inject their original ideas through the CAD system and come away with a good idea of how their creation would perform in the real world. They can determine whether new and untraditional concepts can be viable.

A subdivision of CAD/CAM, computer-aided engineering (CAE), is coming to constitute an area of its own. CAE is mainly concerned with refining and improving the production process; it occurs throughout design and manufacturing. A prototype is designed on the computer, with each internal component tested independently. Once a final product is realized and, again, tested both as an assemblage of components and as a whole, the computerized information is used to define each operation in the automated manufacturing (CAM) process.

One area in which CAE has been applied profitably is network design and management. Networks are groups of computers linked together, usually by a cable, which control the operation of automated machinery like robots in manufacturing and electronic functions such as in telecommunications. Networks permit the more efficient use of processing power, and also the creation of an integrated database that can describe an entire operation.

Computer graphics is combined with database management software to create more powerful network design tools. Engineers use graphics to conceptualize and implement network design. With integrated software, they can draw from a facility database and analyze all significant parameters. Schematic diagrams are generated, and these form the basis for design-rule checking. In addition, engineers use the facility database information created in the design stage to enhance or troubleshoot an existing network. Once a completed design has been entered, the computer generates views of all equipment placements. Different arrangement options can easily be explored.

As information is entered during design, it is sorted into preformatted reports. Parts libraries are created that break down necessary equipment, deriving material description and its cost. Purchase orders can also be automatically created. These job-costing capabilities greatly reduce the time-consuming tasks of job-costing and procurement.

After a network has been fully implemented, facility management software tracks changes and generates operations and inventory reports. Change is inherent in the nature of a network; it must constantly respond to adjustments in operations personnel, market conditions, and technological capability. When the facility database is updated, the new network configuration can be easily described and readily viewed. As a network evolves, this cycle is repeated.

CHEMISTRY

Computers have been utilized in chemistry for many years, with interactive graphics playing a large role in both industry and education. Educationally, it can better display complex processes and concepts than a textbook or blackboard. For research, both academic and industrial, the computer's greatest contribution is in modeling. Chemists are able to view molecular structures from many angles to help determine reactions. Concrete results have already been realized in the synthesis of fungicides and the analysis of viruses.

MEDICINE

Computer graphics has many applications in medicine. One simple way to grasp this range is to visualize the body as a machine and doctors as engineers. CAD systems are used by orthopedists to help with what are basically design problems: the design of artificial joints, bone implants, and prostheses. In surgery, where doctors used to draw on X-rays to plan their operation, they can now use CAD systems to indicate precisely the steps they plan to take.

One medical study used computer graphics to present critical views of muscle and ligament sections that had been removed from cadavers and subjected to performance tests ("Computer-assisted Analysis of Ligament Constraints in the Knee," *Clinical Orthopaedics and Related Research*, Number 196, June, 1985). Medical research utilizes computer graphics in diverse ways, ranging from standard presentations of statistical data to highly complex computer imaging systems with which molecular biologists attempt to unlock the secrets of disease.

A recent innovative application is in the presentation of nutritional information for the critically ill. The computer converts a complex array of nutritional data into a graphic display, which readily indicates how the patient is performing compared to the amount of calories, vitamins, fluids, etc. that he should ideally ingest. The patient is prompted to eat properly to keep his level on a par with his ideal level on the computer display. The nursing staff and the patient's immediate family can quickly ascertain his performance without calculating long lists of chart entries. They are encouraged to be more aware of the patient's nutritional status and to help him strive for optimum levels.

Dentists are using computer graphics both for charting dental data and as presentation aids for directing a patient's preventive routine. Dentists receive greater attention when they graphically depict a patient's problem area and indicate the required oral hygiene. In the near future, dentists will be able to view cavities actually developing in their patients' teeth to motivate preventive care. Since dental data can be kept by the computer with great precision and then telexed virtually around the world, computer graphics may come to play a leading role in forensic dentistry.

While doctors are increasingly utilizing CAD systems to address specific body mechanics, one difficult task that computer graphics is still striving to accomplish is the precise animation of the human body. The human body can be compared to a machine in certain functions, but on the whole it is far more complex than a jet fighter plane. The face is especially complex and is a whole field of study in itself.

Many benefits will accrue as the human body is described more precisely. Doctors will be able to perform stress analysis on the animation just as engineers do with buildings. Borderline surgical cases can be critically evaluated to determine whether an operation is feasible or too dangerous. In addition, surgeons and anethesiologists will be advised what kind of patient response to expect during critical portions of operations. On the educational level, medical students will be able to experiment across a broad latitude and realize a deeper, more detailed understanding of surgical techniques.

Chapter **IX**

Business

Business will comprise the fastest-growing segment of computer graphics through 1990. Graphics will figure centrally in the general computer revolution that is changing the office.

The spectrum of business is too wide to summarize effectively in a job ladder description. Entry-level junior executives generally start in the neighborhood of $20K, and at the top levels of senior management the sky is virtually the limit. For example, the highest-paid CEO in America in 1982, Frederick Smith of Federal Express, earned over $50 million from salary, bonuses, benefits, and stock options.

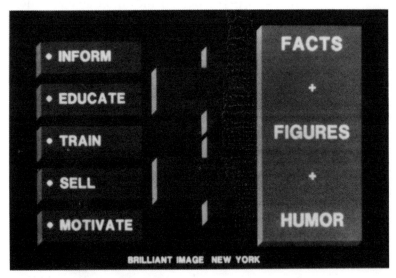

Bold graphics get the message across.

During the 1970s factory productivity jumped 85 percent due to automation, while office productivity lagged behind at 4 percent, laboring under the information explosion that the computer helped to create. As technology becomes more efficient at dealing with this information, automation will progress in the office; it is estimated that 30 to 50 million jobs will be eliminated by the year 2000. Most of this winnowing is expected to occur in middle management, where information is gathered and analyzed for senior managers who make policy decisions. The computer's ability to access and present data and to communicate with other computers in analytical operations will make middle managers more efficient, and in some cases unnecessary. New job functions will also be created as executives spend more time in specialized analysis and less in routine administration.

Computer training already makes an entry-level applicant's résumé more appealing. As the young businessman progresses to the higher salary levels, this knowledge will help to protect him from obsolescence as the office automation crunch develops in

PROJECTED GROWTH FOR BUSINESS
1985–1990

Business is the fastest growing computer graphics applications area.

With 40 percent annual growth, business graphics will increase 553 percent by 1990.

By 1990 40 percent of all microcomputers used in business will be connected in Local Area Networks (LAN's)

1990 will deliver opportunity with a $6 billion business graphics industry.

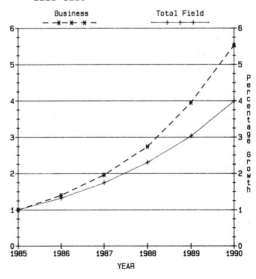

middle management. As computer graphics becomes more and more widely used for data analysis and decision support, the executive with the ability to rapidly assimilate graphic information and marshal graphic support for his own recommendations and point of view will enjoy a powerful tool for career advancement.

Virtually all executive-level positions in business require a bachelor's degree. The MBA degree has become quite common and may even be a prerequisite for some of the most competitive entry-level jobs. Many business schools now offer extensive PC training in business applications, which include graphics.

The successful businessman has traditionally displayed sound judgment, coolness under pressure, and an aptitude for office politics. The businessman of the future will have an increasingly intimate relationship with his computer console; his ability to understand and utilize new technologies will mark him for the rewards of the fast track.

Computer graphics is being used in business to produce materials as presentation aids and, more significantly, to aid in the actual decision-making process. A data explosion has occurred since the computer and its memory became ensconced in the business community some decades ago. The mass of information routinely recorded in numbers and letters has become too large for the human mind to assimilate effectively and efficiently. When rendered graphically, however, such data can be more readily assimilated and understood.

The primary use of graphics in business has traditionally been in design and drafting and in presentation aids. Engineering and manufacturing depend upon graphics, and managers utilize graphics to present information about performance and illustrate strategy. Computer graphics has contributed dynamically to productivity in both of these areas. Computer-aided design (CAD) is now routinely employed by design engineers and draftsmen in the automotive, electronic, and aircraft industries. Similarly, artists can more rapidly and comprehensively create, manipulate, and update graphs, charts, and incorporated text for presentation purposes.

Managers increasingly turn to computer graphics to detect, interpret, and communicate business information that affects the efficient operation of the firm. These graphics are used to describe information, analyze options, and display the evidence that will persuade others to a desired course of action.

Businesses monitor themselves with voluminous reports on subjects such as quality control, productivity, and comparisons between divisions and time spans. Graphics provides an excellent visual summary for this type of recurring information. Data is condensed and made quickly accessible to the manager. Different depth of detail and emphasis of focus are used for different levels of management—regional vs. national, for example.

When a business wishes to evaluate a potential problem or opportunity, computer graphics becomes an analytical tool. The consequences of possible actions can quickly be compared and the best choice made.

After a manager has assimilated summary data, analyzed the situation, and chosen a course of action, he may need to persuade others to his point of view. With computer graphics presentation aids, he can not only show the evidence for his decision but also highlight and emphasize the focus he deems essential. Decision-support graphics is used by product managers, product-line management committees, and project review committees.

In marketing, computer graphics is used to determine site locations and analyze market potential. The computer generates maps that display data for different variables. These maps are produced on transparent mylar can be overlaid on each other and/or on standard road maps to quickly render accurate visual information describing a specific issue or any desired combinations.

For an existing site location, computer graphics is useful for displaying market penetration, sales performance, market share, and market opportunity. If the business is one of a chain of department stores, for example, demographics and topology are utilized to determine how many potential customers are in the area, how accessible the store is to them in transportation and parking, how much disposable income they possess on the average, and how efficiently the store's inventory can be maintained. A competing store in the area would be examined by the same criteria. This information could be directly compared with other member stores of the chain to give management a clearer picture of which parameters were affecting performance and productivity above or below what was expected. All these factors come into play when a business is evaluating potential sites in which to locate a new store. The graphic image provides a detailed comparison of sites and a comprehensive evaluation, leading to the optimum choice. This is especially dynamic when a business determines that the characteristics of a market make site relocation desirable or necessary. On a smaller scale, information maps give salesmen a much better picture of where to concentrate their efforts than a report requiring interpretation of statistics, and the maps can be updated with ease by the computer.

Financial reports often contain charts or graphs to illustrate important relationships. Recently, computer graphic techniques have been adopted by some institutions to display such information as income statements and balance sheets. These graphics resemble horizontal bar charts.

When a business plans for the future, it must always operate on the knowledge it gains from an analysis of past trends. Computer graphics offers a fast way to translate series of statistics into graphic models. Both long-range and short-range performance can be quickly checked against any number of variables. Trend analysis also helps a company determine how well it is performing in different areas.

To summarize, computer graphics is helping business perform more efficiently in many areas by rapidly supplying accurate visual references. Gross amounts of data can be immediately summarized and any errors revealed by inconsistent high or low values. In the same way, deviations from plans or projections are also revealed. Data can be quickly compared to other data. Trends, the direction and magnitude of change over different periods of time, can be readily discerned.

Computer graphics is already affecting the executive's role, both in his day-to-day managerial activity and in his pursuit of career advancement. In the future it is reasonable to expect to see computer graphics centrally involved in nearly all important decision processes, and top-level executives who can demonstrate fluency with graphic representation.

On the day-to-day level, computer graphics focuses the manager's attention. Complementary overlays, detail maps, color-emphasized charts and graphs all enhance his ability to assimilate data. The computer also makes it possible to view data that is virtually up-to-date. The manager can quickly obtain a description of his situation, leaving more time for decision-making. He can view the effects of a decision more quickly, thus increasing his flexibility and his opportunities to react.

Perhaps the most important skill for an executive to possess is the ability to make presentations. For career advancement, he must effectively present his assessment of a situation and his judgment about appropriate action. If his judgments are sound but his presentation skills lacking, his career may languish from inattention, or he may continually lose out to other executives of lesser merit.

Computer graphics profoundly affects an executive's ability to present, to get ahead. Whereas computer graphics is merely efficient for displaying complex data, it is explosive for recommending action—even based on the very same data. This persuasion operates dynamically on two levels: for the mid-level executive trying to get ahead, and for the high-level executive trying to motivate a client.

The mid-level executive with access even to a microcomputer has a tremendous opportunity to present himself. Whenever he needs to demonstrate decision-support materials, he can show up with convincing color graphics. In minutes he can assemble documentation that can enhance his reputation immeasurably. The key benefit of business computer graphics is the same for both the high-level and mid-level executive: The computer can emphasize aspects of data.

The computer offers many ways for the operator to direct attention to information he wishes to give primacy. When an executive can gain assent that a certain factor is truly most important, he can usually expect to have his decision supported. What he has presented, in the most compelling way possible, is precisely his point of view. When he looks at a situation and one thing looms large in his mind as the key to a decision, he has located the factor he needs to emphasize with his graphics.

Business computer graphics is a burgeoning field. Large companies demand tools to help them operate more efficiently, while executives demand tools to enhance their ability to present and communicate. Young companies springing up to fill this demand are discovering great room for creativity and innovation in what has traditionally been considered a dry idea. There is virtually no limit to ways in which information can be depicted. The challenge for artists is to make information as compelling as possible and to avoid repetition. The prospects for growth in this field are enormous: Executives will continually clamor for more hardware, software, and graphic techniques for their companies, for themselves.

Part 3
Career Profiles

Chapter **X**

Interview with a Graphic Design Engineer

Artist Ernie Henrickson designs animations on the Quantel Paint Box and Dubner animation system for NBC News

Q. Let's start with an unfair question: Rate your job on a scale of one to ten.

A. I'd say a respectable seven and a half.

Q. Can you summarize the events of your career that led you to your present position?

A. Yes. I started out in print. I was in advertising for a while, as a traditional graphic artist. I became disenchanted with advertising, and I came to work at NBC roughly eight years ago as a free-lancer, mainly for a change of pace. More accidentally than anything else, it worked out for me. I was happy here. They were happy with my work, they just happened to be hiring at that time, I was put on staff. Since then it's been a case not of the person changing for the job but of the job changing for the person. The technology has been advancing. As the technology advances, the opportunities change. The people who started here as traditional artists have now become quasi-electronic engineers. Well, electronic graphics engineers would be a fairer assessment.

Q. So you did about six years mainly as a traditional graphic artist?

A. No, I did, I'd say, three years in traditional here. We used to use a system called the bismo system, which was rear-screen projection of five by seven chromes. When the ADDA system was first brought in, it was like a watershed event. The

ADDA was the first thing, then we got a switcher, then we got a camera, then various things began to happen. I don't think anyone who has been here for a while thought they were getting into a computer graphics job, because that's not what we came here for. The job changed under us, so to speak. We've ended up being in computer graphics, but we didn't come here for that reason. At least, I didn't. Maybe some people actually did have the foresight. I wasn't one of them.

Q. How do you feel about moving into computers from traditional graphic arts? How do you like the computer? Did you feel you had to keep up initially?

A. No. I like computers. I mess around with stereos and that sort of equipment at home, so I was more than glad to see them come. I like machines. I worked for Dolphin Productions in the early '70s, and they were one of the early computer graphics houses. When I left that to go into print, I always missed the opportunity to mess around with equipment.

Q. Did you have any computer background coming in?

A. No. Other than the time I spent at Dolphin, which was not really a computer job—I was a production assistant there—I had no computer background whatsoever.

Q. How about computers and creativity? Do you feel the machines limit or enhance creativity in any way?

A. Definitely enhance it. Definitely. I've been an artist for many years now and—the Paint Box that I showed you, for instance. Using traditional methods you could spend days airbrushing something and then at the last possible second screw it up. With the Paint Box you can store each step along the way, so if you do make a mistake you go back one step instead of to the beginning. The computers can save limitless amounts of time. For the people who have an affinity for them, they allow you to try many things in a short time. You can turn out broadcast-quality comps on one of these machines in the time it would take you to do a pencil sketch at your desk. They save time; they help my creativity.

Q. Then the efficiency the machines provide really aids creativity?
A. Absolutely.

Q. What's your title?
A. My title is graphic design engineer.

Q. When was the "engineer" part added?
A. About a year ago, when we switched unions from a traditional film artists' union to the union that represents most of NBC's employees. Before we made that change, my title was assistant graphics director. When the union entered the picture, everyone's job title changed. Those of us who operate equipment and are also graphic designers are called graphic design engineers. People in the department who do not operate any equipment and who do only traditional work are called graphic designers.

Q. What do they do with their work, bring it to design engineers like you?
A. Yes.

Q. Do you have straight engineers who only work the machines?
A. Yes, we do. We have a limited number now of engineers whose specialty is the machines. They do ADDA only, or switcher only, jobs that don't involve creativity. Jobs that are closely supervised by a graphic artist. Nothing in the department is put on air that isn't designed and art-directed by a graphic design engineer.

Q. Can you give a brief description of your duties?
A. I work right now for a man who does pretapes for Nightly News. A pretape is concerned with a story that can be pre-planned, that isn't breaking news. It could be a story on the economy, for instance, a long-term story. We develop concepts, ideas, and animations for these advance stories. My day is spent doing animations on the Dubner, doing storyboards for that animation, getting these things approved. Then I work with another artist who does Paint Box. Generally that person will be doing backgrounds for the anima-

tions I'm doing. We work together, the two of us as a team, and we create graphic displays for future stories, not for day-of-air stories. Currently, however, I have to say I'm not assigned to that. I've spent the past six weeks being a production design engineer for Nightly News, which is somewhat of an unusual move for me.

Q. Is most of the information you produce charts and maps, or do you do a lot of pictorial rendering?

A. We do a lot of pictorial stuff. If you watch Nightly News you can see the results of our work. I'd say it's roughly fifty-fifty pictorial—talking about work load only. The appearance would be that it can't be fifty-fifty, it's mostly pictures. But as far as work load is concerned, I'd say it's divided fifty-fifty between maps, charts, and that kind of graphic display and what you would consider traditional graphics. There are more graphics in the show than maps and displays, but the maps and displays take a lot of work and time.

Q. Are the computer graphics more efficient for illustrating a story than, for instance, stock film footage?

A. Well, yes. We've used them quite often in situations where there is no stock film footage. For instance, there was a plane crash in California. We did the plane coming down—it actually landed without a tail or something—as a computer animation. Recently, we did Reagan's Star Wars missile system as a computer animation.

Q. That sounds like fun?

A. Oh, yeah. It was interesting also, because we made full use of the Grass Valley Switcher, which I haven't seen done before. We actually, I think, used all of the equipment to its full potential. That was full-scale, full-blown animation. It resembled the NASA animations, which are considered by many to be among the best in the business.

Q. How about stress? Does this occupation entail heavy pressure?

A. Yes. Working in a news organization is always heavy pressure. We're under a daily deadline. Unlike other forms of graphic arts that only demand perfection, they demand perfection on time here. And I'm not talking about weekly deadlines or monthly deadlines; we're talking about daily and even hourly deadlines. Most of these people come in at 11 in the morning, and our show airs at 6:30. We have to complete a news show, from start to finish, from concept to finished art, in about 7 hours—counting everyone's lunch, so we're talking about very heavy pressure.

Q. Do you feel that the schedule ever taxes your health?

A. Not in any serious way, but as I said before, this is the news business. I was here when Three Mile Island went up, and I was here for three days. I didn't leave this building for four days. I was sleeping on the floor. We couldn't leave. Nuclear energy was a hobby of mine; I had read a lot about it and that became known to the people in the newsroom. I became their graphics expert on nuclear technology. So I couldn't leave. I was very tired, and I think I slept for three days after that. There are people here who work the night shift—the graveyard shift from midnight to eight in the morning, and their health is greatly taxed by what they are doing. In general, the only thing I can say about health is that the hours are long. It's a twenty-four-hour business; we all know that when we get into it.

Q. Is it fair to assume that most people take the night shift hoping to get onto the day shift eventually?

A. Oh, yeah. I have known some people who actually like the night shift. In fact, I knew one person who left the company because he was transferred to days and couldn't get back on the night shift. But the majority, yes. Nobody wants to work midnight to eight, or at least virtually nobody.

Q. How about geographic location—did you want to work in Manhattan?

A. I was born and raised in New York. It never occurred to me to work anywhere else.

Q. Do you think geographic location is a limiting factor for the field in general?

A. Yes. There are certain major markets right now. I think that as the technology advances, expands, as the companies lower the prices of the equipment, as it becomes more generally available, you'll be able to work anywhere. But right now the work we're doing is only being done in New York and possibly Los Angeles and San Francisco. I know that Turner is quite advanced down in Atlanta with CNN. I'd say the field is limited right now to the major markets.

Q. So you're happy working in New York?

A. Yes, although I'd work in San Francisco in a minute.

Q. What kind of salary range are you in?

A. Over forty thousand dollars a year.

Q. How about benefits?

A. The benefits are excellent here. This is a major corporation; the benefits couldn't be better.

Q. How do you think you fare compared to practitioners of traditional design?

A. That's kind of hard to say. I think the short answer would be that I do a lot better than your traditional graphic artist. There are some graphic artists who develop an extremely stable and wide-ranging clientele, but they often have to put in weekends, to put in nights. They're putting in a lot more hours than I am to earn the same money. I would say that in general this is a very lucrative job. There's more money to be made elsewhere, certainly; but there's also a lot less. I'd say that the majority of graphic artists make less than we do here.

Q. How about mobility into other fields? If you wanted to move on from here or if you were laid off, how do you think you would fare on the job market?

A. Probably pretty well. I must say that I've been here eight years, so I haven't really been out looking in the market, but...

Q. You could conceivably go to other news organizations or to computer animation production companies?

A. Umm, yeah, I would think so. Also, the technology has reached the stage, at least here in Network, where a lot of us have been trained on the Grass Valley Switcher and the ADDA, and those devices have actually transcended graphics. At this point, someone who is trained as a graphic design engineer at the network level could actually get a job as a technical director elsewhere and do on-air switching, which is not a graphics job at all. It means that you have to know the switcher. We recently had a man leave for a cable station management position. We've had other people leave and go to work for editing houses as technicians—very highly paid technicians. I'd say the prospects are pretty good. Unfortunately, as I said before, there is a very limited market for what we do as graphic designers, and there are many people within those major markets who do what we do, and many more who want to do what we do. I would say that if I were in charge of another network's news, rather than hiring someone like me for fifty thousand dollars a year, I'd get a trainee for little more than half of that, teach him everything that I would know coming into the job, and put him to work. So I think that movement within the market is somewhat limited.

Q. On the other hand, you've also mentioned the time pressure. A news director might need someone to go to work *now*, and not have the luxury of time to train someone.
A. Possibly, but never underestimate how budget-conscious the networks are.

Q. Do you especially like or dislike a particular piece of the equipment you work with?
A. Yes. Personally, my all-time favorite is the Paint Box. I think it holds the entire future, or at least the foreseeable future of this business.

Q. Anything you dislike?
A. Not really. Although, let me add one qualification. The Dubner is a wonderful device, but if the people who own the Grass Valley group, who now own Dubner, want to stay in business and stay competitive, they should make that machine more user-friendly. I love it, I've been using it for a long time, and I've had no problems with it, but I can see that as a tool it is going to become obsolete if they don't get it up-to-date.

Q. You mean make it easier to use?

A. Yes.

Q. How about the training you needed to use the computers? Was that provided on the job?

A. Yes.

Q. What kind of person trained you? A technician?

A. For Dubner it was interesting. The machine was bought before they had anyone to train, to handle training. Dubner, the company, was booked solid at that time. So the machine just appeared in the department one night like a mushroom, and a manual was there beside it. Those of us who were interested sat down with the manual and just sort of figured it out. I reached a point at which I just didn't know enough to understand what the manual was talking about, and at that point NBC sent me to Dubner and I was trained by one of the founders of Dubner.

Q. So you're actually in the first generation of this kind of computer graphics artist?

A. At NBC I am.

Q. If someone came in today to join the department and be trained, would it be you or someone like you who would train him?

A. Yes, either myself, or one other man who has been doing this longer than I have.

Q. Should a person interested in this kind of work try to get similar training on the outside?

A. Yes. If you can train on any of this equipment on the outside, you should do it. However, one warning about that. There are devices, such as the Dubner, on which you can take training, but if you don't continually have your hands on that equipment you will forget everything you know in no time. So I would say yes, a person should try to get training on the outside, but he should also make every effort to work. Even if he has to work for free, he should try to keep his hands on the equipment.

Q. How about personal qualities a person should possess? What kind of attitude suits this kind of work?

A. If a person is going to do this he must have a definite sense of what he is doing himself, yet—it's strange—since this is a corporate environment, he must be able to play that game too. It's a two-edged sword. To be a good graphic designer you have to have your own vision. To be able to survive in this place you have to be willing to subjugate that vision to someone else's vision. You have to have a pretty open mind to work here. This is a news organization, so you hear things that aren't generally known and you also hear things that you may personally disagree with. You can find yourself arguing all day long if you get into the nitty-gritty of what it is you're actually illustrating. You also need a great deal of patience to work here, and a willingness to put up with a lot of sacrifices in your personal life that maybe your friends aren't putting up with. It's a twenty-four-hour business, and they can tell you tomorrow that you're now working from four in the morning until noon.

Q. Just like that?

A. Yes, just like that.

Q. Is the ability to work with other people necessary?

A. Yes. Everything here is a team effort. Even someone like me; when I'm working on Dubner I'm generally in that room alone, but I'm not working alone. I'm working with a producer, with another technician who's doing something on the character generator, with someone on the Paint Box. Communication is very important in this business. You can't get your instructions and go lock yourself in a room because things change constantly and you'll find when you walk out that what you've got isn't what they want.

Q. Would you characterize the general atmosphere as mainly pleasant or somewhat antagonistic?

A. It's a highly political environment, as any environment would be when you've got a limited number of jobs and an unlimited number of people who want them. The schools are turning out thousands of students each year; to a lot of them this is the top of the heap. Certainly there are people I enjoy working with . . . it is political. That's all I really want to say about it.

Q. What's the most challenging thing about your work?
A. When they come to you with something impossible and you do it. That's the most challenging thing. That happens a lot.

Q. For example?
A. Someone will come to you at four in the afternoon and say, "You know that animation you've been working on for the last three weeks, that you just finished yesterday? We've decided to use it tonight; however, it's all wrong and you have to do it over." You end up doing that animation that took you three weeks to do, in a modified version, in the space of two hours. It may not be the prettiest thing you ever put on air, but it's there. It's on air. There's no black up there.

Q. It sounds like that might also be the most rewarding aspect of your work?
A. For me it is.

Q. What about the three-week finished piece?
A. Actually, it depends probably on temperament. My temperament is geared so that I like to be . . . I've been here a long time. If you've been here maybe six months, then I imagine the three-week piece would be more rewarding—turning out a beautiful piece would be a challenge. I know what I can turn out in three weeks. I've done it often. The challenge for me is to see how beautiful a piece I can turn out in three hours.

Q. Like quick chess?
A. Yeah.

Q. What's your most tiresome task?
A. That's a good question. I've never really thought about that.

Q. That's a good answer in itself. Most jobs seem to entail some sort of tedium or dull routine. Is there anything you find particularly frustrating?
A. There are many frustrations. I think it's part of the business. It can be frustrating from beginning to end. As I said, you have to be able to subjugate your visions to someone else's. That in itself is frustrating. We constantly deal with nonar-

tists here who due to their position in the hierarchy of the company—and rightly so—it's their call what goes on air.

Q. They don't have to know art to know what they like?

A. Yeah. We've had producers say, "Never use green. I hate green, I never want to see green." So you do a baseball story and the outfield is this blue lawn. There are producers in this building who are notorious for their eccentricity, and a lot of the time—since ours is the most tightly controlled aspect of the business—we're the ones who suffer that eccentricity.

Q. How competitive is your position?

A. Very, very competitive.

Q. So if someone has essentially sound credentials, is that enough, or do they need a little extra?

A. Yes, you need a little more. Credentials are fine, but they're not everything. One of the managers in our department is fond of saying that he interviewed three people in one day and each one had exactly the same work on his reel. So those are credentials, but which one of the three do you give the job to?

Q. You mean identical work, not the same kind of work?

A. Yes, identical work. That happens a lot in this business; it's a cooperative business. It's conceivable that I and the person I work most closely with could show our portfolios and they would be identical because every piece we've done, we've done together. Credentials are certainly a way in the door—someone without them isn't even going to get an interview. But what you need after credentials is a good portfolio. You need excellent skills, and nowadays they're looking for technically oriented people.

Q. Comparing a very strong, creative portfolio to technical skills, where do you think the weight would fall? Is their importance equal?

A. Nowadays? . . . It's strange, because we're just going through a changing period. If you had asked me that a year ago, I would have said forget about the technical stuff, you can always learn that; but now I would say that it's fifty-fifty. It depends on what they're looking for at the moment. The graphics department is changing now to the extent that you have creative people working side by side with people who aren't creative at all. They're only there to lend technical expertise. They tell you what you can do with a particular machine, for instance. Some of us are becoming hybrids. We're talented artists who are being eased into being technically oriented also. So let me just say that it certainly wouldn't hurt to have a technical background.

Q. How about working with the technicians? Is tension generated there, or is it a team-effort kind of spirit?

A. I would say in general that it's a good relationship. This is, as I mentioned, a union operation. The engineers have been in that union a lot longer than the graphic artists, so that many of them, although performing an operation of subordinate importance to a graphic artist, are earning more money than that graphic artist. So you can have the art director of Nightly News earning less money than the man he's telling what to do.

Q. Do the engineers resent the power of the artists at all?

A. There has been a period of that. You've walked in here at an interesting time because so much is changing. There's a certain amount of resentment about that, yes. There's resentment on both sides. I wouldn't say it's anything terrifically serious; it will all work itself out eventually... but there are inequities, let me say, in the structure.

Q. What advice would you give to a student interested in this field?

A. I would tell him, assuming that he's an artist, to go to the best school he can. If computer courses are available, by all means take them; and if no computer courses are available, find a place where he can take some. Put your hands on everything you can that has to do with computers. If a person is primarily computer-oriented, I would advise him to stay away from keyboard-operated devices as much as possible and try to learn some of the more esoteric devices, some of the more...

Q. Interactive?

A. Yeah. So he can be useful in a computer graphics situation. The line is fast disappearing between artist and nonartist in this business, because so much can be done by an artist and then put into a computer. Someone else can take it from there, someone who doesn't have to have an esthetic.

Q. How about that? Do you ever worry about a computer person, or a technician who knows how to operate the machines, calling up the pictures even though he doesn't have—

A. We've had that for years. That's one of the inequities I was speaking about. Ever since the ADDA equipment was brought into the office. Initially, since that was union work and we were not of that union, we did all of the work and took it into the computer room and fed it to the great god of ADDA, at which point a technician stored the stuff and played it back. So, effectively, the artist was out of the picture once the stuff was in the computer. If the graphic was great, it was common to hear the director say, "Great graphic" and the technician say, "Gee, thanks." If the director said, "That's a terrible looking graphic," the technician would say, "I'll tell the graphic artist."

Q. Do the machines actually make it possible for a person who can't paint, can't draw, and has no color sensibility to produce graphics?

A. Well, let's say that he could participate.

Q. With a lousy graphic?

A. Well...no. I've seen some people with absolutely no art training who can do good work. I think they're beginning to notice around here that people who have done editing have developed some kind of an esthetic that at least allows them to do animations, and in conjunction with a talented graphic artist they can turn out beautiful animations. They know how to make things move, and the artist knows what to make.

Q. That's interesting—people with backgrounds in different

mediums meeting at a point provided by the new technology. Looking at a person who's just a little farther down the road, who's a couple of years out of school—what kind of things might you ideally hope to see on his résumé?

A. The ideal résumé for someone wanting to come into computer graphics, I would think, would include a good solid art background, plus a good solid computer background. A good way to get experience is to work for a production company, where things have to be done quickly and have to be done right. A certain amount of waste is allowed here that isn't allowed out there, because this is an internal department. We're part of a larger company, and things sometimes slip. We call it government work, which you're not allowed to do outside, and that's a good solid training ground. Outside, they have to account for every single nickel. They're not on some large company budget that is buried in the overall payroll office. I would say that that's a good bit of experience to have on your résumé, that you've worked in production somewhere.

Q. I assume that someone would have to have a strong, creative portfolio to get hired. But as the technical and artistic fields begin to merge, I'm wondering whether a student might be better advised to aggressively seek out and concentrate on computer courses to balance his creativity with technological knowledge—even at the risk of getting a lower cumulative average?

A. Umm, yes, I would think so. Of course ideally the cume will stay up anyway, but I do think that the more exposure there is to computers, the better. In addition to a portfolio these days, it's almost standard for someone to have a reel of some sort—now it's video tape; it used to be film. You also have to have flat artwork. A lot of people think they can walk into a place with a reel only, but as I mentioned before, three people can walk in with the same reel. What will decide a manager's mind on whom to choose will be what he sees in the book [portfolio]. If the flat artwork is, say, the comps or storyboard for what's on that reel, then that person would probably have the best shot at getting the job.

Q. How are opportunities for women in the field?

A. Excellent. I don't think sex is a factor at all. It doesn't seem to be.

Q. How about age? Say someone making a career change got some training and wanted to come into the field, would age be a discriminating factor?

A. That's very hard to say, largely because the field tends to be fairly young. I'm in my thirties, most of the people here are somewhere between their middle twenties and late thirties. We do have one man who started several years ago who's in his fifties. He had a background in calligraphy, he decided one day he wanted to go into television—and they hired him. Among the things we do is create fonts. Calligraphers can be quite useful for that. He was hired, he's being trained for various things. He's the only person I know of who actually showed up at the door who was not young. We've had older people, but they'd been working here for ten years or more. In other words they got older here. I don't think I have an answer.

Q. Well, let me put it this way. Do you think age might be held against someone? Say someone forty years old wanted entry-level?

A. I think that if someone were willing to take entry level he'd probably get it. If he were qualified and were willing to take the money and the position—entry level really isn't fun for anyone. My personal opinion is that it wouldn't be a factor.

Q. How about your ultimate goals and your career progression? Where do you think you might end up; where would you like to end up?

A. Well, for anyone in this business, from a technician to probably the president, the ideal is to become a consultant. You're more or less self-motivating then; it's your own business. Everyone wants his own business. This is very lucrative, but what I think I'd eventually like to do is start up or own a production company of my own. And I don't just mean graphics, I mean live shooting and all that— everything, from beginning to end. However, I may be too lazy for that.

Q. What do you think about the future of the field of computer graphics itself?

A. It's the way it's going. From now on I think we're going to see that traditional graphics—even in print—are eroding more and more. There are computerized typesetting machines; there have been for years, and they are getting more and more advanced. I think in general that computers are going to take over this field. There's a thing called "bubble-memory" now that's on the horizon, which I don't fully understand, but from what I do understand it utilizes liquids as a storage medium. Supposedly that's going to revolutionize the business even more. It's going to make computers five, seven, ten times faster than they are now. To most people, computers are instantaneous right now, and we're shaving down into nanoseconds with this. I don't know if it's just a conceit of design engineers that we have that kind of speed, or if it's necessary, but I think that computers are where it's all going, and it's not going to go backwards. As long as there is electricity to power them, I think computers are where it's going.

Q. Is there a question I should have asked you?

A. I don't know...I don't get interviewed a lot.

Q. So we'll just assume that there probably is. Anything to add, or say in summary?

A. Yeah. If anyone's coming into this business, into television, I would say the one thing they should realize before they get into it is that if you're not willing to make sacrifices you're going to be very disappointed. I consider this business a yuppies' delight...There's a lot of people out there who are willing to work virtually any number of hours, any number of shifts, and they're just gung-ho from the word go. They are going to go far. Anyone who wants a reasonable social life is going to have to compromise his work goals. It's not the kind of thing where you can make those sacrifices for a year or two and have it over with. It continues throughout your career here. It's a rough business in that way, and anyone thinking of getting into it should know that from the beginning. We get a lot of people who come to work here and leave in a very few months because they didn't really know what they were getting into. They thought it was glamorous, and—it's not glamorous. Sure, you can run into some pretty big celebrities in the hallway, but that really doesn't make your day. That's the most minor part of this business, which is hard work, long hours. It's largely unrewarding except financially. Rarely does someone come up to you and say, "That was a great job." Generally, what is considered to be a compliment is when no one says anything about it so you know that it was okay.

I would say that the most important thing to know for a person coming in is that it is a sacrificial business. You have to be willing to give up a lot. If you're not willing, you should just stay away. And the other thing is that once you are in here, you should never coast for a moment. You have to stay up with everything or you fall behind very quickly. You have to be constantly training yourself; the networks themselves have sort of sketchy training programs. If you want to know something, you have to make it your business to find out about it. Go to the person who does know and look over his shoulder and watch.

Q. You have to be very inner-directed?
A. Yes, you have to be inner-directed and you have to be self-motivating, or self-starting or whatever they call it these days. It's up to you to stay on top, because people are constantly coming in from somewhere else who may be more advanced than you are. They know lots of things you don't know. If you want to stay up, you've got to know what they know. It's rough.

Chapter **XI**

Interview with a Computer Graphics Entrepreneur

Jerry Cahn is president of Brilliant Image, a young microcomputer graphics company that creates innovative business graphics.

Q. What's Brilliant Image all about?
A. Brilliant Image is a unique company. We're a full-service microcomputer-based firm that specializes in making professional presentations. We offer a range of services starting from slide producing, designing them and doing them on our

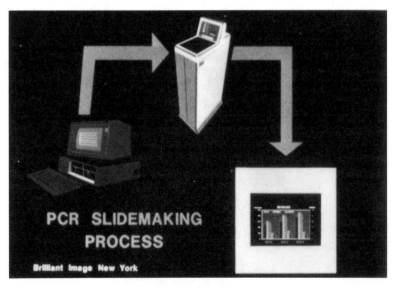

A computer generated image that shows how these images are made.

own computer using our own artists, to helping corporate executives do it by upgrading their IBM PCs, XTs, whatever, into full-service workstations. Now what makes us unique is that we back them up with a range of services that isn't offered by anyone else in this industry. We have design expertise behind the production, test capacity behind the training, hardware expertise, installation of hardware, software consulting, free-lance artists—you name it. The purpose of this is very simple: We're a communication graphics firm. We like to think of ourselves as doing *communication* graphics, and we're trying to help corporate America communicate better by using graphics; whatever it takes to help them, we'll do.

Q. You use entirely microcomputers?

A. All micros. If a company has a mini or mainframe, they learn how to download to micros. In fact, we may introduce a new product just to help them do that.

Q. How central are the computers to the operation of the company? Is their importance greater than that of design?

A. No, people are at the center of the company, no matter what industry you're in. Even if you're making robots. Remember that.

Q. How long has the company been in operation?

A. We will be operational two years next month.

Q. How did the company come to be started?

A. It's kind of unique in that my partner and I are both business people, really. I'm a lawyer and a psychologist, so I have a very different background, but I wanted to do something with microcomputers. My partner was an officer in a bank and he wanted to do something with microcomputers, so we started asking ourselves questions. One of the things that had bothered me—from when I used to work on Capitol Hill—was that lobbying groups that I felt deserved a lot of money were never getting it because they didn't do good presentations. My partner had just done a major slide show for a major bank for which he paid through the nose. He did it with a computer firm using minis and he thought

"Shouldn't it be faster, better, cheaper?" It wasn't. So we did an analysis and we realized what everyone was doing wrong, so we started Brilliant Image. Then, by using artists and artists' expertise, and our business acumen, we discovered that—the tip of the market had barely been touched. That was really our goal, to start breaking open the market. At this point I think we're at .5 percent of the market; 99.5 percent is still ripe for the plucking.

Q. Did you go for any computer graphics training yourself?
A. No.

Q. So you stay mainly on the business side?
A. Oh, no. I design on the systems. In fact I just did a slide show for Pratt on the designer's point of view. My partner, who is also a business person, produced some of the best slides that have been published from Brilliant Image. We practice countless hours on the system, and read and learn. It's a combination of practice, reading, and learning, and we work with artists who help us. A lot of the other people around here are artists, and they have the art skills. We come up with a design and they show us what we're doing wrong and how to do it right. But on the general side, I'm not on the system anymore; neither is he.

Q. Do you use any people in a purely technical capacity?
A. For designing work they are artists. You really have to be an artist to be on the system now. It's not like the system in the early days when Mike and I did it; now you have to be an artist. You don't have to be a computer artist; you just have to be an artist who likes computers. That's the only criterion I can give you. That and a personality I look for. Innovative, entrepreneurial, excited by a new technology, willing to challenge what everyone says can't be done, things like that.

Q. So you look for people who exhibit entrepreneurial personality traits?
A. You got it. That's what's built the product here—we've gone from four to thirty people in two years.

Q. What kinds of people do you recruit?
A. It depends on the division, really.

Q. Well, for instance, do you take people coming out of the schools with backgrounds in computer graphics?

A. Not necessarily. We have, I'd say, for each person we hire, about ten applicants—ten that I would seriously consider, that is. We might have hundreds that I won't consider. We prefer people with computer expertise—strongly prefer, I should add—but it's not required. If I have a really solid artist with great skills and that's what I'm looking for at the time, I'll hire him.

Q. How much weight falls on the side of technical expertise as opposed to a creative portfolio?

A. The creative is more important.

Q. So, for instance, if A is an excellent artist and B is a good artist with a solid technical background, you would choose A?

A. The answer to that depends upon what you're looking for at a particular time. For example, I get a lot of word slides to do. I don't need a creative artist for that. So if it turns out that I need, right now, more people to handle the meat and potatoes, I'll go with the person who is fast on the machines. If it turns out that I'm working on a new medium, as we are with our new video slide, and I need more design capabilities, I'll go with the creative artist.

Q. The general atmosphere here seems rather hectic?

A. It's more than hectic; we're growing very fast, it's *exciting*. There's an air of excitement; when you walk in you can feel it. That's part of what we're all about.

Q. Do you see computer graphics as a growing career area?

A. I think so. In fact, it will grow because we're going to make it grow.

Q. How about money? Do you think computer graphics will prove more lucrative than traditional graphic arts?

A. I can't answer that. I don't know what the other side offers; I'm not a graphic artist by profession. I think the market is there, and I think it's opening for a different group of people. I think the best way of explaining it is that .5 versus 99.5 concept—of course the numbers aren't precise, they're abstract, but they are indicative. It used to be that if I wanted to do a show of any sort I would need a budget, and it would be expensive. I'd go to my art department or outside to somebody, to a service bureau, and they'd charge me a lot of money to do a show.

So the number of people who could make that kind of request is very limited. Microcomputer graphics is changing all that. Now I can be in control of a company and just love playing with Lotus and love throwing some graphics together and conceptualizing a problem for myself, and I realize—because we're all part of the Yuppie generation, and we're all trying to make it through—that if I can not only analyze the data but present it somewhat well, I can get a raise, a promotion, and that's what it's really all about in this industry. So what's happening is that business people who were never ever before involved with presentations are suddenly going to be doing them. So the challenge for the graphic artist is to work for the right kinds of companies who understand that that's where the real marketplace is.

For instance, when we planned to open our second division in which we upgrade IBMs to workstations some people said "You're crazy, you're taking business away from us! Right now we get service bureau work, you just ripped away your service bureau." I said, "No way." Down the road, the world's going to be full of people doing the basic slides themselves—simple bars, pies, texts. What's important for an artist is to let that person so it himself! Then, after a little while, take that same person and say "Isn't it boring, what you're doing? Isn't it boring to show the same word slide, the same bar chart, fifteen times over: The audience doesn't notice the content anymore because it's just changing the title, it's the same format. What you need to do is spice it up, do it exciting, use the designer's eye, use pictures."

So suddenly there's a market that's going to grow in this side of the industry, for people to design the creative side to those presentations that never even existed before. It's a whole new thing that's opening, and companies like Brilliant Image are unique because we're going to be that bridge. We're going to help them set it up with all the creative and artistic capability here to back them up. It's a teamwork approach that we're creating. It's a whole new world, and it's a question of your orientation and motivation. The understanding that you may have to do a lot of boring business slides to get to the exciting stuff, but you'll get to the exciting stuff.

Just to give you a statistic: Supposedly 60 to 65 percent of all business slides are composed of words, 30 to 35 percent bar charts and things like that, and 5 to 10 percent is exciting. Brilliant Image—in the production work that we do the numbers are totally opposite. We do maybe 20 to 25 percent text, 30 to 35 percent bar charts and the rest is sophisticated bar charts with 3D, special effects and high-class stuff like Fred Flintstone on the wall there. [Points to a graphic on the wall in which the cartoon character draws attention to the most significant factor on an information display.] That's the kind of stuff we do now, and we can do it because we spent time educating clients. Which, again, is something a graphic artist doesn't do. By teaming up as we have here with trainers and business professionals, we educate them on how effective graphics will say more than plain bar charts will.

Q. Do you have any kind of progression plan for making charts that deal with repetitive information continue to be interesting? For instance, a phase one developed through to a phase ten?

A. It's a question of the artist and the storyboard and what works. No, we don't have a prototype or any rigid structure. I like every artist to stay creative and react to each situation. We have brought in two cartoonists to add that kind of feature. Again, two years ago we wouldn't have thought of that. It's a whole new industry.

Q. Do you think computer graphics artists have mobility into other fields?

A. That's a function of the person. We have some people who are very narrow-minded, and the answer is no. For example, selling and educating are divided by a fine line. If you know how to convince a client to choose a better slide show, that's both sales and education. We have artists who like working with people, and I've trained them to do that. So they spend most of their time designing and they're never on the computer anymore. They're out in the field working with a client; they're bringing in gorgeous shows as a result. I have other people who hate dealing with people, so they're great at the console. I think the industry is wide enough that "different strokes for different folks" really applies.

Q. How about opportunities for women?

A. There's no sex discrimination or race discrimination in this industry. There's only one discrimination: Either you're good or you're not.

Q. Do you get any people coming in who are in mid-career change, people in their thirties and forties?

A. The answer is yes. We don't discriminate about age, either. To be honest, I couldn't tell you where everyone started— their individual histories. Most of the artists I think started as artists, but we have people over forty who could have done other things in their lives previously. One of my top-notch artists worked with administrative activities. She had the knack, and we let her play with the computers until we discovered that she had talent as an artist; now she's a computer artist. She's one of the best here.

Q. What advice would you give a student interested in entering this field?

A. Make the decision early on that you want to get into computers. Develop good skills. Don't get pulled in by schools that advertise with lots of glitzy ads but teach you on the wrong kinds of equipment. The biggest problem I find in New York is that there are a number of good schools, but some of them are doing a disservice to students. Let me give you an example. There's a school that's running a major set of promotions right now—I won't tell you which school. It's training people on equipment that virtually no computer graphics firms use. I know because I just donated a machine that I couldn't use anymore and they're training students on it! I think a student going to that school is being disserved.

Another school is training people on a piece of machinery— we've hired at least two people from there, and they had an advantage because they had some computer training, but they still had to be trained from scratch. Why? Because the system they were trained on is not one used in production by most companies.

The critical thing is to find schools that are working with a production company, that train students to think commercially, and train them on machines that are used commercially. I think one of the biggest flaws in the schools is that they don't understand that. Every one of them should be at my doorstep trying to buy my systems, and working with us. It's the most inexpensive business graphics system out there. Every day I'm placing more systems in big companies proportionately, given the resources of this company, than many other system vendors. But the schools aren't buying these systems; rather they buy paints and other less commercially viable systems. As a result, the students come in unqualified despite having taken one or several courses at popular schools. Nobody uses a Commodore or Atari in a commercial environment. It just doesn't have the resolution or the horsepower. I think that's a real problem. Students have to be very careful about that. There's nothing wrong with the schools saying that they're going to get fundamental skills, exposure to computers, but they're not going to be working on "real" systems.

Another thing is for students to understand what they want. Fine art is gorgeous, and a fine artist will love it, but it's not commercially viable. The hardest thing I have to do is show an artist that. I'm not saying that it won't ever be viable, but it won't be for a long time—and it may never be, because of limitations in the way that kind of software is written. So I think they have to understand that if they want to be fine artists, computers are probably not the best route to go at this time. If they want to be commercially oriented artists, computers are the way to go, but they must focus on that. And be creative.

There are all kinds of new opportunities, and they should try to explore some of them. We run an internship program, which gives students a real chance to learn. I'd say half the people in this company have been interns at some point. One of our senior managers was an intern less than a year ago. It's a tremendous growth opportunity, both for this company and for the interns.

Q. What does the internship program entail—summers, year-round?

A. It's year-round; it's a rigid program, you have to put in a minimum of fifteen to twenty hours a week. It's generally a four-month period, although if you work more hours it can be less. There's no salary, and there's no guarantee of a job. But for that period of time you really get to work on a concerted project. You get a real sense of dedication because you work with everyone else and you become part of the team. Sometimes, if you're working on an important project that becomes good enough—which is why we'd have chosen it—it becomes something we can use to market and it can lead to a job. There's no guarantee of a job, I'm explicit about that at all times; but I think about 80 percent of our interns have obtained jobs here, which says something.

Q. When they've finished their internship they'll obviously have something good for their résumé. Will they also have something for their book?

A. Depending on what they've been doing. Remember, not all artists work on the systems. Some prefer to do other things. But, yes, they do get samples. By all means.

Q. What kind of elements would you ideally like to see on the résumé of someone coming in the door?

A. If I have an ideal, it would be to have some computer graphics experience. I do look for that. And some of the schools do work with some of the systems. Also, an internship in a company like this. I get many calls from schools, which seems to indicate that I'm one of the heaviest users of interns in the city. Some real-world experience, I'd also like to see. And then there's that personality factor again, that entrepreneurship and desire to achieve, willingness to move one step forward, that I want in people.

Q. What's the most frustrating thing about working in computer graphics?

A. There are two levels, I guess. One is explaining to the public what computer graphics is. People seem to assume that you've got this black box and you press a button and then everything happens.

Q. But it's not magic?

A. It's not magic, and that's a real problem, explaining that it won't do everything. The second part is teaching artists what computers really do. I just did a major presentation on the designer's point of view, and I brought in a new illustrator to create copy. He did illustrations that were totally incompatible with how a computer works. So now we've realized that before we use an illustrator we've got to let him spend some time on the machine and see for himself that some illustrations don't convert. Artists also have to recognize that we have audiences. We have 16.7 million colors to choose from. An artist can go crazy with that amount.

Q. 16.7 million colors—is that a precise figure?

A. Actually, it's a derivation of 256 x 256 x 256. It's a color panel combination. Business professionals are used to using very limited numbers of colors, maybe only black, yellow, and blue. So if you give this person ten colors you're blowing him away. Why are you wasting someone else's time worrying about a hue and a saturation and a luminance of .297? That's a real problem when a new artist comes in, and we have to educate him. It really doesn't matter, and it's not that big a difference, because the business professional all too often will use boring word slides. What we need to do is spend less time worrying about the specifics of the derivation of a color and more time showing professionals that the power of the computer should be communication. I think that's the final point I'd like to make. I think artists have to understand what art's for. It's a communication device. They tend to forget that. Art, in computers at least, up to this point is "commercial art"; it's not for "art's sake." It's for communication's sake, and that's the hard part for everybody to understand—that it's communication consistently across the board.

Q. You seem to be implying that the ability to communicate is in itself very creative?

A. Yes. I think I'd like to see that taught more in school.

Q. What's the most challenging or exciting thing?

A. The industry itself. It's a booming industry; if you're creative you can grab a big piece of it. And to have the right people around you is the nicest part about it.

Q. Anything to add or say in summary?

A. Not really. But I do think this industry requires that students spend a lot of time doing their homework about what the current state-of-the-art is, and what the world really is about, each and every time. If they don't follow through, they're going to fall, again, to using antiquated machines in out-of-touch schools.

Q. That seems like a problem that could recur quite frequently as the technology advances. How might a student check up on the business? For instance, to know when a school is inaccurate in asserting that its machines will provide the necessary training?

A. I think if I were a student I would immediately go to some of the major trade magazines that list companies like us and take a summer off and be an intern. Or take a semester off after the senior year. Volunteer the time to get an education. You know, it has always struck me as incredible for people not to recognize that when you go to school you pay, and yet when someone offers you a free chance to learn in the real world-environment—and you're learning something more practical than you're going to get anywhere else—there's an attitude that if you don't get paid, you can't do it. You pay to go to school, and you may get very little out of it. I'm astounded at letters I get from former interns. I had a student who later got a master's degree, and she sent me a postcard saying that she had learned more in the two semesters she spent in her internship than she did in earning the master's. I think that sums it up.

Q. How about a student getting on the phone and just calling a number of companies?

A. And?

Q. And saying, "I'm thinking about going to this school and are their systems relevant to the marketplace?"

A. You're not going to get the time of day. You see how busy it is around here. I mean, I'm friendly, but I'm hard to reach. The schools should be doing this themselves. I went out to one school, to do my public service, to do that sort of thing, but it wasn't well organized. I'm not sure I'd be willing to do it again. But their approach was the right approach, and that's why I did it.

Q. So the students really have to carry the responsibility to find the schools that offer up-to-date programs?

A. Right. Maybe it will change, but it's always up to the student to take the initiative.

Chapter **XII**

Interview with an Educator

Martin Bressler is chairman of the Art Department at the New York Institute of Technology and coordinates the computer graphics program for the Graduate School of Communication Arts.

Q. Perhaps we should attempt to tie our subject down a little with a definition: What is computer graphics?
A. Computer graphics is creating images, various images, by electronic means. The electronic means consists of the com-

Student work from the Art Department at the New York Institute of Technology.

puter at this point. So it's a new kind of artist's tool in creating graphics.

Q. Can you tell me a little about what you do here?

A. I wear several hats. I'm chairman of the Art Department— we run a program in design graphics, interior design, fine arts—and I also coordinate the computer graphics program for the Graduate School of Communication Arts. I oversee, look at portfolios, review students' work, and so on.

Q. What kind of facilities do you use?

A. For computer graphics we have various facilities. We deal with an Images system, which is a computer that was created by the school, NYIT; they did the software and the hardware configuration. And we have a lab with Images I and Images II—basically the same computer. Images II is a newer and less expensive version. We also have a lab with microcomputers—Apples, Commodores—and we're trying to offer the students some work with microcomputers as well. So we go from microcomputers to what we call a mini-computer, which is a self-contained unit, but the Images is larger than the microcomputer, more powerful.

Q. That's the one that was made here?

A. That's right. That's the one that the school developed and also sells.

Q. I noticed that the New School offers a certificate in micro-computer graphics. Is there any program here that might roughly correspond?

A. Well, we don't offer a certificate, no. We offer on the gradu-ate level the opportunity for a student to earn a master's degree in the communication arts, specializing in computer graphics.

Q. What about undergraduates—could a student major in, or strongly emphasize, computer graphics?

A. An undergraduate would most likely major in design graph-ics. Then he would have a series of courses in computer graphics in his junior and senior years. The degree is in design graphics.

Q. So a student could place an emphasis on utilizing the computer?

A. Right.

Q. May I ask what the computer graphics program is intended to accomplish, how it developed, and where it's going?

A. Well, it's still developing. We are adding to it, trying to discover what the needs of the students are. On one level, the most important thing is to introduce the student to this new painting tool—how do you use it? It's more complicated, and yet simpler, than using oil paints. You have to learn the vocabulary, you have to have the hand-eye coordination. You come into the program already being a designer, either upperclassman or graduate student. We don't want to have to teach fundamentals of art.

Q. So you want students to be developed as artists before they come to the machine?

A. Right. We want them to know what we call the design elements, and to be able to sit down and accomplish that kind of thing. Our purpose is to teach them a new tool with which to accomplish it, a tool that can be very powerful because it's very fast and does many things. That's the intent. The program also opens an awareness of what's available in the art world, what's out there, things they are not aware of. The computers have been popularized, you hear a great deal about them, but there are many things the student may have seen, on TV for instance, that they don't realize are done by the computer. Many of those logos that turn and spin are done by computer—many of them by our school, actually. Many students had no idea that was computer-generated art.

Q. How long has the program been operating?

A. The actual program, teaching, has only been around about three years. Certain things were done on a teaching level before that, but as a full program it's very recent.

Q. Do you emphasize different tracks, more technical versus more artistic?

A. I would say more artistic. We now have a video hookup, so we're dumping into the video studio and trying to interplay a paint image from the computer into a video tape and see how it works with live video. This is very new, just happening, and the students are very excited about it. It opens the possibility for students in design graphics to become aware of video production. In the degree map, the undergraduates must take one TV production course, so they have a little bit of that, but this opens up a whole new experience. In the graduate school, students with an art background who have never had video are required to take a video course, a production course. We're very excited, because it really has changed their thinking. They may have come in thinking about using the computer just for illustration; they now see a whole new potential for it.

Q. In a word, motion?

A. It would add motion, yes. The video gives a new dimension. In business graphics, these are programs that we will probably be instituting.

Q. How about computer-aided design and engineering applications?

A. Well, we expect to buy a computer with the capability to do all that. We want to see what the students will need. We have an interior design program, and a computer that will do frames and then manipulate them in ways that would be used in engineering technology, or industrial design, would be very appropriate. The students could take the same program, for instance, and do interior dimensions. So we want to do that for the undergraduate student who has the potential for it. This equipment would be an on-the-market computer; it would be moving away from the Images.

Q. How about the future of the program? Do you think it will grow, perhaps move into other areas?

A. A long-range possibility that we would like to have would be the capability for animation, three-dimensional animation. An awful lot of equipment would be needed for that. I don't know if we even have the space in this building to run it completely, but we could perhaps begin it and then take it someplace like Central Islip where we have more room, and let the students do a more or less concentrated finishing there. I think the president of the school would like it if we could offer some sort of animation.

Q. So you feel in general that it will grow?
A. My feeling is that it will grow. It's been growing all along.

Q. Do you think that might be a common trend nationwide, or limited to the major urban centers?
A. Yes, I think it's happening or will soon be happening in all the schools. I don't think many of them will make the heavy investment that we have in the Images, which are expensive. We were lucky because the school created it. The research lab made the equipment and the computer graphics laboratory sells it, but we're all part of the family, so we have equipment that you would not find at other schools.

Q. So the computer lab does things like logos and sells them in the business marketplace?
A. They do things like production. They create things that they feel are challenging, things that make them test their skills. They're way overloaded, but they'll do things that they feel merit their attention.

Q. That must be a major resource?
A. They've been a major resource.

Q. What sorts of attitudes and abilities seem to predispose a student to an interest in computer graphics?
A. The graduate student is an art student—90 percent of them have BFAs in some aspect of art, either design graphics or fine arts. There's no question that they've been studying art for four years; many of them come from the art colleges.

Q. Do they seem like average art students, or do they seem to have a technical bent?
A. I think they have the art student bent. But, you see, the art students are very curious people. And we do have students who want more of the technical. We ran a pilot program out in Old Westbury offering a computer language course for computer graphics specialists who wanted technical infor-

mation. I don't know the results of the course because it's still in progress, but it does show that there is technical interest, and we want to do the same thing here. If it is successful, if the bugs are out of it, we want to offer the course here next spring. Once the students get involved, you see, there are enough of them who want to know the technical aspect. Once they get involved with video, they want to know parts of the camera and how the different parts work together. What is encouraging to me is that it has opened up to students from primarily an art background the experience of a whole new world. If your area is painting, when you use the computer you're suddenly interfacing with video and learning a new language.

Q. What about ability? What do they need to get into the program?

A. On the graduate level they have to qualify in grade average and transcripts. It's applying to a graduate school.

Q. Is it highly competitive?

A. It's enough, yes. They need a B average. If they don't have a B average they have to take GREs. So it's competitive on that level. And then there's a portfolio review. I look at the portfolios, and I have an associate who also reviews them.

Q. So they have to have grades, but you also want to see good evidence of creative ability?

A. They have to be art students, yes.

Q. It seems that technical ability is becoming more and more important. How do you balance a person's ability to walk into a job and sit down and use the machines with the creativity he demonstrates in his portfolio?

A. Well, I think our track record has been pretty good in placing students. Being in New York, there are a lot of companies, both small and large, with computers. My philosophy —and it seems to be proving itself—is that the knowledge that you pick up, for instance on the Images system, bleeds over to another system. It might have a different menu, it might use different names, but the process is the same. You're going to touch, you're going to move the pen across the palette, touch buttons or whatever is necessary. So that allows you to use other systems. The work on the micros, the personal computers, also allows them that knowledge.

Q. Where do students go from here? What kinds of places do they work in?

A. Well, there are various related companies using computers. Some computer companies using Genigraphics are willing to train students in using the Genigraphic computers, which create slides, business slides mainly. That opens up one area. Some production houses are using computers. They might not use Images; they might use Quantel Paint Box or something, and our student fits into that if the student is good and the company is willing to put in the time for training. What I'm suggesting is that the time necessary for training our students on any kind of equipment is much less than to train someone without that exposure.

Q. What can someone do who can't go through the whole program but wants to get some hands-on experience?

A. It's difficult. The graduate school admits what we call special students. They are allowed to take certain courses on the basis of space availability. They're allowed to take up to nine credits, and some of those credits could be on the computer. The other thing we have offered is a professional workshop. It's for no credit, and it's open to anybody, although we do like to see a portfolio.

Q. Well, that sounds like a good opportunity.

A. Yes. They are sort of crash courses—very intense—and we offer them during the summer with a day format and a night format.

Q. Grades. Since computer graphics is so new, might it be more worthwhile for a student to get his hands on as much equipment as he can than trying to engineer a 4.0 cume?

A. In graduate school there's no grade below a B. You're going to get all As and Bs; otherwise you're not cutting it.

Q. Do you think someone with a computer graphics background fares better than a person with a traditional graphics background when he goes on the job market?

A. I don't think so. I think it would really depend on the person's situation and the interview. There's no question, certainly, that a company with computers might be interested in talking to someone with experience in computers, and that might weigh in favor. But you know, not all companies have computers. A company without a computer might be interested in seeing the work and might like the work, but they'll want to know the other skills. They'll want to see what else the person is presenting. If the work is illustration, they'll want to see the illustrations.

Q. When a student graduates and goes to seek a job, what is he armed with? Presumably he has a portfolio of flat work?
A. Yes.

Q. How about some kind of reel?
A. He could have a reel.

Q. How about the résumé itself? I would think that it would read a little better, be a little more impressive technically?
A. I would agree. I think anyone would be interested in that dimension, but again, it's not going to get the student the job unless it meets the needs of the company. If the company is heavily entrenched in computers, then it certainly might help.

Q. Are there any obstacles that have to be overcome in the study of computer graphics, anything that is particularly frustrating?
A. Sure. They don't get enough time on the computer. For them that's the worst. I sympathize, but I cannot do much about it. We figure out a system of how many hours we feel a student should have, can have—a system that is feasible and workable—and that's the reality. I think we have seventy students in the graduate program as well as about a dozen undergraduates, and the numbers are always growing. So we really have a busy schedule. The other thing is breakdowns. For instance, the computers will not function in 80+ temperatures. We do have air conditioning for the computers, but it's not that great, and when the temperature goes up, I wait for them to crash. So students lose work, and we lose time. I had to extend one semester an extra week so students could

make up time. I think the greatest frustration for the students is time. Sometimes they want to stay there all day.

Q. What about the most rewarding thing?

A. Well, for me the most rewarding thing is when somebody gets a job, or is well placed, or wins an award. To see that they really are working well and understanding what the computer can do—that's rewarding.

Q. How did you happen to move into computer graphics?

A. The nature of the school is this: We have a center called the Media and Arts Center, in which are communication arts and fine arts. As chairman of fine arts, it was logical to get into computer graphics. It was natural that I would be involved in supervising the art. I was trained on the computer, I was excited by it, and I enjoy it. I find that the more I use it, the more I don't know. There are so many little subtleties it can do.

Q. What's the most exciting thing about it?

A. I think the most exciting thing is that within a very short time—even a half hour—you can have a completed piece of artwork that will look quite good. With an idea that you have, you can reach a resolution in a short time. And not only can you bring it to resolution, but you can instantly change it, do something else. And not only that, but you can store it in memory and recall it at any time.

Q. So the speed and flexibility frees you from being caught in your work as you go along?

A. Right. Not only can you change it, but you can also store the original that you're changing. You can work out all kinds of permutations; you can change what you just changed and have all the changes. So you have the original piece of artwork and all the changes, whereas if you made changes in a traditional piece of artwork, the original would be lost. So this gives a new dimension.

Q. What advice would you give to someone who is seeking computer graphics training with the idea of eventually working in the field?

A. Well, the first thing I would say is: Why do you want it? What is it going to do for you? Usually the first thing I say to people is what do you want from computer graphics?

Q. Okay, then what would be a good or a bad answer to that question?

A. Well, I think a bad answer would be, well—if you think it's going to make you an artist, forget it. It's not. An answer that I feel would be decent enough is people in career change who seriously want to open up their experience to other kinds of things, and they see it as a possible way to earn an income. I think that a serious kind of investigation is essential.

Q. Anything else I should have asked you?

A. I think you've covered everything.

Q. Anything you'd like to add, or say in summary?

A. I will say something. My own ego says that the computer will never replace the artist. The computer is only a tool. Some people might be frightened at the idea of it. I think that kind of fear is unwarranted.

Q. Well, do you have to be a little more aggressive? It seems a lot different from the kind of creating you do when you, say, go home and work on a drawing all night. Here, someone is hovering over you shoulder looking at his watch.

A. Well, yes. One thing we try to impress on the student is "Hey! You've got a project due; this is $250, $300 an hour computer time. You've got to get that done." It's true that we give them a kind of pressure, but we do it because that's the real world.

Q. So the limited time element really provides good real-world training—very real and untheoretical deadlines?

A. Yes. And a company is not going to pay for extra computer time if it isn't absolutely needed.

Chapter XIII

Interview with an Analytical Engineer

Giulio Maleci is a product marketing manager for Gen-
Rad in San Francisco, California. He uses computer graphics to
test mechanical structures and electrical circuits.

Q. What is your title?
A. Product marketing manager.

Q. What is your company's name?
A. GenRad; it used to be General Radio. Let me tell you briefly
   what GenRad does. It does not do graphics particularly; it
   tests equipment, things like electronic equipment and different types of structures.

Q. So GenRad checks structures and electronic circuitry?
A. Yes.

Q. How do you use computer graphics to do that?
A. In the division I work in we test mechanical structures. That
   could be anything from a board to an airplane or aircraft.
   We need to acquire data from the structure itself to graphically represent the results of the testing. So we have a simplified model of the structure, and we see how the structure
   deformates under certain load conditions and certain environmental stresses. Part of this involves animating the structure on the screen so we can look at the different
   movements. In real life this would happen so fast that there
   is no way the human eye could pick them up. So with the

transducers, through the graphical representation, we slow down this kind of movement, and the changes in amplitude; at that point it's all inside a computer model, so you can, for example, expand an area of the structure or change the speed of the animation. So the engineer can really understand what's happening in the structure, and from there he can try to design a better structure or to modify the existing structure. It's excellent for troubleshooting.

Q. What kind of equipment do you use?
A. We are based on a Digital computer. We ride the front end; that is the part that acquires the data and converts the data into a digital format that the computer can analyze. After that we have our own board that will do the animation. It's a microprocessor, a dedicated microprocessor that can modify and do the graphics functions. It will only be available on graphics terminals at much higher costs, because so many graphics terminals are made for general purposes. We need a specific type of graphics; we are very much interested in animation and the capability to modify all these parameters like speed and amplitude. We are not really interested in added graphics capabilities, so we developed our own graphics board.

Q. How accurately does it describe reality? Can you identify a problem and say that the structure definitely will fail?
A. Yes. From a graphics point of view it's very interesting. I identify three kinds of graphics boards, what I call low resolution, medium resolution and high resolution. We do not need a particularly high resolution (1,024 x 1,024, or in that range). We do have 640 x 400, what I call medium resolution, graphics. After that you have the low resolution 140, 180 x 400, which you find in the personal computer type of graphics board. So, in our case, the emphasis is more on this capability, the animation, than it is on the actual resolution itself. For other applications, such as a purely mathematical model like finite-element analysis or solid geometric modeling, high resolution is a must. We do interface a lot with computers, because we want to correlate analysis data with test data. So even if we do not do the analysis part, if we do

not need that capability in the graphics terminal, we do a lot of times correlate the results. So we attach our computer to a Digital, Vax, or MicroVax computer, for example, and on that kind of computer you use very high-resolution terminals like Lexidata, Megatech—there are hundreds of terminals that can be used as graphics stations. We do compare results from analysis and tests for correlation purposes. So the results from tests can be used in three major modes. One is troubleshooting, another is correlation with analysis data to ensure that we did the right analysis, and finally testing components to be used in analysis. In all three applications the graphics part is very important.

Color is even more important for complicated structures. Presently we do not have color capability because it would be too complicated to have the animations in color. As far as I know, few companies can afford to do that; they are very expensive terminals, around $20,000. A new generation of terminals will soon be introduced, and apparently for around $10,000 or $8,000—less than half the cost of what was available in 1985—they will do those kinds of performances.

Q. How long have you been involved with—is it accurate to call it CAD/CAM?

A. The terms are a little complicated. There are three, CAD, CAM, and what we call CAE. CAD is a computer-animated graphics that is used instead of a pencil and a drawing board; it's an automation of that particular task. CAM is computer-aided manufacturing, an automated manufacturing task, doing the numerical control of the machines and so on. And also passing the drawings from a design stage to manufacturing with the tolerances and everything that is needed to view the data that goes on the numerical control machine to make the part involved. Computer-aided engineering (CAE) is a little different because it involves all the different tasks: manufacturing, design, drawing. It's more up-front in a way. That means that instead of using a pen and paper to design something, you design everything in the computer right from the beginning. So you have different software that can take you from a very simple sketch, basic geometric components assembled together, to building complicated structures. From there, you refine your model through all the different steps, and you go automatically from conceptual design to CAD, then through CAM, and through all the engineering steps that function to accomplish the manufacturing process.

Q. And you are in the CAE stage, the engineering stage?
A. That's exactly true. Either that or, once the product is built, in checking the product. So mainly our product is used up front. When you design a prototype, basically, you start with components. Let's take a car, for example—which is a very good example. When you want to design a new car, usually you don't have completely new parts. The first step will be to take competitive cars, or existing cars within the company, and test them to find out what you do like, what you do not like, and what is presently available. That's one of the first ways in which you can use testing, and again, the graphics part is very important. Afterward, when you understand that, you start designing analytically and developing all your models. Once you develop the models of components of the structure, like the engine, the door, and single components, you go one step further. You build that component and test it to check with the analysis. At that point, if you are satisfied with all the components, you assemble the prototype and test it. If you are satisfied with that, you go further into the manufacturing stage. Once you are in the manufacturing stage you check again, because each product is different from the others; there are never two identical products, but all the products stay within tolerances that you define at the design level. So in all these stages the graphic part is instrumental, especially in the design stage.

Q. Can you give a quick sketch of the events of your career that brought you to this point?
A. I started as a mechanical engineer, and I went into consulting after I had done some special courses, mainly dynamics. After that I went into a consulting company. I stayed in the

consulting position for a while, and I really used this tool. After that I moved here and specialized because I knew the applications. I wanted to make a contribution in designing new products.

Q. How long have you been involved with computer graphics? Did you start with a design board?

A. No. I always came with them—from a user point of view, not a designer point of view. Basically I've been a user of computer graphics since my college years. I needed computer graphics to understand what my model was doing, and so on. So I've never been involved with building computer graphics, with the engineering. I've been involved with the definition. From a user point of view I can say how many colors are needed, or what the resolution should be, which kinds of commands are easy to use. We have some special keyboard buttons, and I can use them.

Q. Did you do any structural analysis testing, before you used the computer graphics?

A. I started using computer graphics when I was in college, to represent my models and projects. When I came out I continued using computer graphics through the consulting stage of my career.

Q. Did you want to keep using graphics in your career, or did things just naturally evolve that way?

A. I think that the capability of the computer to represent reality—particularly for engineering purposes—is the reason we are using the graphics. And computer graphics can help communicate not only technical information, but also marketing information. For example, it can represent market share, market trends, or even, more simply, it can produce transparencies for overlays. We make a lot of use of a program that's on an IBM PCAT that's called Draw and Graph; it helps us to make all the slides we need for our presentations, technical presentations and product introductions. We have a camera that takes pictures directly from the monitor, so that what is on the screen can be photographed without actually having to take a picture of the screen; we can take a picture without having to put the camera in front of the screen, with all the reflection and distortion from the curvature. So there are two new cameras that can take the picture directly from the IBM PC.

Q. And now that picture is ready to be processed as art?
A. Right. This is used very much at every level and in all kinds of companies. You don't have to be an engineering company to use this kind of tool. There is no limit to the ways graphics can be used for communicating ideas and concepts, and for communicating information. It would be very difficult and expensive to do it all by hand.

Q. What kind of attitudes would suit a person for this kind of work?
A. An attitude that I think is very common in the high tech professions is self-motivation. You need to want to get something for yourself, to be enthusiastic about the work you do, and to try always to discover new things. If you think about what computer graphics was just five years ago—it's unbelievable. It was primitive. And now you see computer graphics workstations with power that was virtually unimaginable even two years ago. For about a third or a fifth of the cost. And this trend is common not just to computer graphics but to the whole computer industry, hardware and software. So I would say that the attitudes of computer graphics people are similar to those of the rest of the people in the high tech community.

Q. How competitive would you say the field is?
A. I would say extremely competitive. All these fields are innovative, and they attract a lot of smart people because the work is not repetitive, not boring. It's a field where you can contribute and see the effect of your contribution. It is also a field that has a lot of potential: You can make money or go into some kind of entrepreneurial operation. But still it is conceivable that if you have good ideas with a limited amount of money you can really do a lot of things. And therefore the field is very competitive. The guy who comes up with new ideas finds it easy to sell. When the field is high

technology, it's performance that matters, and therefore you always have a chance to have new people coming into the field, if they have something better. Even if a competing company has better distribution, better advertising and so on, if the product is better, that's what will sell. Now this is all relative, not absolute judgment, but it is one of the reasons the field is so competitive. Over time, it is the companies with the better products as well as financial and marketing skill that will be able to survive.

Q. What advice would you give a student who wishes eventually to enter the field of computer-aided engineering?

A. Well, first of all he has to be in the right place. He has to be at a university that has solid ties with industry. There's very little benefit in working in a purely academic environment, where there is no dynamic exchange. It's important to choose a university that has been proven, not just to follow that industry, but to complement what cannot be done in that industry, like long-term research. Second, try to go with a company that is interested in development. As an investment—and I think this is true for all areas of business, not just this one—when you come out of college, it's better to go with a company that has some kind of research programs, where you can learn a lot. Then later on, maybe, it could be good to go with a company where you could see what the leaders in the field are doing, because by then you would have a good understanding of what is involved. So there are two things: first finding the right training at the university level, and second finding a company that does research, so that you can continue to learn.

Q. Do you think computer graphics has any effect on creativity in technical design, as compared to traditional methods?

A. That's a good question, because there has been a lot of debate about how much your concentration on learning the computers limits your creativity. I don't think it really limits creativity, because the trend is to make the computer much more user-friendly. You have to recognize two different applications in computer graphics. One is to help to automate a task that is very time-consuming. In this case there is no effect upon creativity because there was no creativity in the first place. It's just for making things easier and faster and of higher quality. In the other case, in the design stage, there can be a problem only if the system is very difficult to use, if the user has to expend a lot of effort in understanding how the system works, instead of trying to think what he wants to get out of the system. Now, after thirty years, the programs are much easier to use, the hardware is much faster, easier, and cheaper; so there is definitely a trend toward making it easy to use the computer, so that you can even talk into the computer, instead of issuing commands and so forth. I don't know exactly when this will come about, but a lot of work is being done on this and on artificial intelligence. Artificial intelligence is not something that exists in a separate domain; it will affect the whole computer industry in interfacing with users and making the computers easy to use. It's difficult to say when all this will happen, but I would say that computers will always be intended as helping tools. They help to get information out of a repetitive mode, a boring mode, and help make it more creative. I think that is definitely the trend.

Q. Does the computer allow the designer more latitude for experimentation? In the design of a car, for example, could a designer experiment with a new shape and then test it on the computer, rather than going all the way to the prototype stage and facing costly consequences for failure?

A. Well, you always have to go to the prototype stage. But in the past, even five years ago, you had to go through series of prototypes, perhaps eleven series of prototypes. Everything was done through testing. It took forever, and was highly expensive, because for every modification you had to modify the manufacturing capability. What you do with computers, both in the testing and in the design stage, is checking. Right now, I think there are only three or four series of prototypes. Prototype testing is not something that you can really replace. It will always be there. There's no way they will let a plane fly just because the computer said it would fly. But with the computer, you won't find that the tests tell you what is wrong with your structure; the tests will tell you that you did a good job. Instead of a lot of repetition and trial and error, you just wait for confirmation from tests that you did a good job. That saves a lot, but tests will never be replaced. They will always be an integral part of the development of any electronic or mechanical structure.

Q. Do you think the computer graphics element enhances mobility, the ability to switch fields?

A. Definitely. I think computer graphics is one of the most advanced skills that you need to have in a computer environment. You can move horizontally into different disciplines that are related to computers once you know how to interface with computers, to interface with the memory. All those different elements are integral parts to all computer graphics people. For example, there is a person in our company who is responsible for a computer graphics board. He started as a professor's research assistant at a university, and from there he went to work for a computer company in a different role, until recently, when he had all of this kind of experience. Then he went to work at MegaTech, which is one of the big computer graphics companies, and from there, after working as part of a team designing computer graphics terminals, he came to our company. He's now a leader of the project for our computer graphics board.

Q. How about age? Would you say that computer graphics is a good field for someone wanting to make a mid-life career change?

A. I don't know. Here in the Bay area, the average age is really young. All of the people who are working, with the exception of a few technical directors, probably average between thirty and thirty-two years old. Not directly out of college, but young.

Q. Young, flexible people?

A. Definitely. Because the companies are very competitive, and there is a lot of change. People have to be willing to be very involved. This is one of the centers for computer graphics, along with LA and Boston. Those are the three major areas where engineering is done.

Q. How about working conditions? Are the hours long and hard?
A. Definitely.

Q. How about pressure?
A. Again, the person has to be self-motivated. Not just in computer graphics, but in any computer-related firm. The rewards come not because someone else pushes you, but because the environment pushes you.

Q. Do you think having the computer graphics knowledge has an effect on how much money you make?
A. Yes. They are higher-paying jobs. There are longer hours and less security, but the pay is better and there is more satisfaction. So you have to make a trade. If you want security, you should work for... well, the government. If you want challenge, computer graphics, and high technology, is a good area.

Q. How do you view CAE as an area of career opportunity at the present time?
A. I think that right now there are very good opportunities. There's a great deal of activity here in the Bay area.

Q. Is a BS degree enough, or is an advanced degree necessary?
A. I would say that for computer graphics specifically, you need some advanced capabilities. If you want to be a project leader. If you just want to learn, with a BS you can learn in a company, but it will take longer and you won't get as fast a start on your career. So it all depends on whether you want to be part of a team, or whether you want to be a team leader. If you want to be a leader, I think a master's would be preferable. Traditionally there are not a lot of people with the master's in high technology, but I think it would be a good thing to have.

Q. How do you think this opportunity will carry on into the future?
A. It's very difficult to say—I wish I *could* say what's going to happen in the future! In the short term I would definitely say that I see a lot of opportunity. In the longer term I can't predict what changes might occur.

Q. Do you see any technical occupations being threatened as computer graphics develops?

A. Every time you automate a process, like CAD, you make if faster, make it better. Therefore a certain number will lose out; if they're not willing to learn the new techniques they will find themselves becoming obsolescent. And, unfortunately, that does sometimes occur. So you must have flexibility in your work. Traditionally, companies are pretty good about trying to retain people, with a few exceptions.

Q. In there anything you would like to say in closing?

A. Yes. As a general thing, I would say that computer graphics is really an integral part of computers. Graphic workstations have the computer built in, and there is more and more emphasis on having everything integrated. The knowledge it takes to operate computers and to operate computer graphics is similar. It's the same kind of environment, the same kind of skills, the same kind of people, the same kind of attitudes, even, I think, the same kinds of salaries. I don't know how much you want to differentiate between computer graphics versus a career in computers. From an applications standpoint graphics can be a lot of different things, but I think from a conceptual standpoint it's part of a career in science.

Chapter **XIV**

Interview with a Desktop Publisher

Richard Shen is Creative Director of Unlimited Grafix Ink, an electronic publishing and graphic design firm.

Q. What is desktop publishing?
A. Desktop publishing is a design tool that enables designers to produce printed materials with the use of a computer. With desktop publishing, printed materials can be created with greater efficiency than ever before; it has brought design costs down and shortened production time.

That is very important in today's world, which is getting faster every day as technology advances. It used to take weeks to send a letter across the continent; today, with the use of a facsimile machine, it takes only a few minutes. With that kind of speed in communication, people need to be able to get their messages and ideas out faster. Desktop publishing is the answer to that need.

Q. Why is it called desktop publishing?
A. Because originally a computer and a laser printer were all that was needed to print a small book or a brochure. Those could fit on a tabletop or "desktop." Today the technology has advanced, and many additions have been made to improve desktop publishing. Now a complex system can fill a small room, but that small room full of technology is equivalent to what used to fill a whole building.

Q. Why do you like being a desktop publisher?

A. Using a computer has made designing fun. A designer is always limited by the amount of time available to work on a project, and by the resources available. Using traditional design methods, experimentation with different ideas can be very expensive, and each idea can take a long time to develop. With desktop publishing, designers can try different design ideas by just typing in some commands or moving the mouse, and the result can be seen right away.

Q. What types of things have you designed, and what do you like working on the best?

A. I have designed magazines, books, menus, packages, and illustrations, to name just a few. I enjoy the variety of projects that I can work on with the computer. The computer lets me explore different ideas and formats. My imagination is the only limit. I enjoy working on different projects because each one challenges me to look at things in a new way, to create something that is useful and beautiful.

Q. Why do you prefer desktop publishing to the traditional forms of design?

A. Traditionally, a designer goes through many steps before a piece is ready to be printed. With desktop publishing many of those steps are simplified, or even eliminated.

Let's say the project is a menu design for "Frank's Hot Dogs." First the designer gathers all the information to be included in the menu. Then he makes some quick sketches of what the menu could look like. These small sketches are called *thumbnails*. They would probably range from some ideas for listing the items at "Frank's" with a few illustrations, to more complex ideas such as a menu that looks like a hot dog.

Drawing thumbnails is also the first step for a desktop publisher. There is no getting around this important "thinking" step.

Once the designer has a few thumbnails that look good, he or she does more detailed drawings. These are usually done with markers and are called *marker comps*. The designer tries to make these drawings look as much like the final piece as possible. He or she hand draws the more important words, such as: "Frank's Specialties" or "Super Sundaes," and indicates where the *body copy* should be. Body copy is the text that describes the menu items.

That is where the computer starts to make things easier. Instead of hand drawing the words, everything can be typed into the computer. The type can then be reorganized as many times as necessary for each of the different comps. It can be made larger or smaller and can be changed to many different styles with a few clicks or a stroke of the mouse, instead of hours of hand drawing and copying. Also, illustrations can be drawn directly on the computer or put into the computer by a process called *scanning*. These illustrations can then be moved around and changed. With all of these options, the desktop publisher can change his or her mind several times without having to redraw. Also, the final comp looks more like the final piece than the traditional designer's marker comp does.

The next step is to have Frank pick the menu design he likes best (let's say he likes the hot dogshape). Once a design is chosen, it is time to make the *mechanical*. The mechanical looks just like the final menu, except that it is in black and white. It is what the printer will use for printing the menu.

The mechanical stage is the busy time for the traditional designer. The drawing of the hot dog for the cover needs to be done just right. It will be drawn large and then made smaller on a *stat* machine so that any imperfections will be lost and the drawing will look sharper. The type needs to be specified, or *spec'd*. The designer writes out all the words he needs and specs the size and style. That is sent to a typesetter, who prints everything as the designer spec'd it out. When the designer gets back the stat and the type, it is time to cut and paste. Using a sharp knife and a straightedge, the illustration and each section of type are cut out and pasted down, with hot wax or rubber cement, onto thick illustration board. This can take days.

The desktop publisher has it easier at this step. The hot dog picture may need to be worked on, and the type may need changing around, but all that can be done right on the computer. Once everything has been checked and is ready to go, the desktop publisher has the final piece run out on a *Linotron machine*. This will be of the same quality as the typesetting, but all the type and the illustration will be in the right places so no cutting is needed. It can be pasted in one piece onto a board, and it's ready to go. This usually takes about one day.

Q. Are there any other benefits to using desktop publishing?

A. Yes. One of the biggest problems with design is last-minute changes and corrections. With traditional design methods, that means going back to the typesetter, possibly several times. With desktop publishing, changes can be made directly on the computer. Type can be changed easily, and even the illustration can be modified. For example, if Frank decides that he would like ketchup on the hot dog illustration instead of mustard, the yellow can be changed to red right on the computer.

Q. What do you find to be the biggest problems with desktop publishing?

A. Computers, like any complex machinery, break down occasionally. When that happens there is trouble, especially during a project. It's as if a race car were to break down during a race.

Q. What do you do when that happens?

A. First I diagnose the problem, and then I try to solve it myself. If I cannot, I hire a technician to fix the computer. I also have *backups*. As a car carries a spare tire, I have backup equipment to help me through a crisis. Things can get pretty crazy at times if the computer is not working as it should, but I have found that the best way to deal with any problem, whether it be with a computer or a person, is to stay calm. Panic never helps. You need to think clearly to solve a problem.

Q. What types of experience would be beneficial toward a career in desktop publishing?

A. Any art or design classes are a good starting place. It is important to learn the basics of design theory and composition. It is not enough simply to know how the computer works.

   Also, jump at any chance to work on a school paper or other publication. Even if the publication is not produced with desktop publishing, it is helpful to understand traditional methods of layout.

And of course, computer courses would be helpful. Many colleges and universities now offer courses in desktop publishing.

Q. What did you study at college?

A. Desktop publishing was just making its start when I was at school, but Macintosh computers were available, and I made the most of my time in the computer lab. I was studying graphic design and advertising, both of which I find extremely helpful now, because desktop publishing is only a tool. A painter needs to know how to use a brush and how to compose a picture. A desktop publisher needs to know how to use a computer, and how to design.

Q. Do you have to be a "computer genius" to do desktop publishing?

A. No. Computers are now very *user-friendly*. Many of the tedious and repetitive *computer commands* have been reduced to the click of a mouse. That does not mean you will master desktop publishing in one day. Like learning to do anything, you need time and practice to be good at working on the computer. You do not have to be a genius; all you need is the desire to learn.

Glossary

algorithm Procedure typically composed of mathematical functions for performing a task, such as removing a hidden line from the display of a three-dimensional solid object.

aliasing Undesirable visual effects in computer-generated images caused by improper sampling techniques. The most common effect is a jagged edge along object boundaries.

alphanumeric Alphabet letters, numbers, or symbols.

anti-aliasing A filtering technique that gives the appearance of even lines and edges on a raster display. Intermediate intensities between adjacent pixels reduce the "staircasing" effect of sloped lines.

CAD/CAM Computer-aided design and drafting/computer-aided manufacturing.

coordinates Ordered set of absolute or relative data values that specify a location in the Cartesian coordinate system.

CPU Central processing unit. Mainframe, the central processor of a computer system, containing the arithmetic unit and logic. (In a microcomputer, the CPU is often on a single chip called a microprocessor).

CRT Cathode ray tube, type of graphic display that produces an image by directing a beam of electrons to activate a phosphor-coated surface in a vacuum tube.

cursor Highlighted indicator on the display screen that indicates where the information input will be displayed.

digital to analog converter (DAC) Interface that converts digital data (numbers) into analog data (images).

digitizer Vector graphic input device that scans an existing image by registering X, Y coordinates at significant intervals.

direct view storage tube (DVST)   Graphic display device that does not need to be refreshed because the phosphors excited by the direct beam remain illuminated.

database   Collection of related integrated files that provide an application-independent model of a real-world data structure.

frame buffer   Memory device that stores the contents of an image pixel by pixel. Frame buffers refresh a raster image. Sometimes they incorporate local processing ability and can be used to update memory. The "depth" of the frame buffer is the number of bits per pixel, which determines how many colors or intensities can be displayed.

electronic mail   Automatic display of alphanumeric or graphic information at a remote location.

font   Complete set of the characters and symbols that make up one size of a typeface.

graphic input device   Device such as a digitizer, which gives the computer the points that make up an image in such a way that the image can be stored, reconstructed, displayed, or manipulated.

interactive   Immediate response to input. User can modify or manipulate a graphic image directly, in real time.

light pen   Input device consisting of a stylus with a photocell in its tip that communicates graphic information to a CRT.

matrix printer   Printer that forms images from dots that conform to a matrix unit. The more dots, the higher the image's resolution.

microcomputer   Small computer containing a microprocessor, input and display devices, and memory in one unit. Also called personal computer.

microprocessor   Single chip or integrated circuit containing the entire central processing unit.

monitor   Display device in an interactive graphics system.

nanosecond   One billionth of a second.

persistence   Length of time an image produced on a display device by activated phosphors remains bright and clear.

pixel   Picture cell. Smallest unit on the display screen of a raster scan CRT that can be stored, displayed, or addressed.

plotter   Hard copy output device that draws an image. Most common are pen plotters, electrostatic plotters, ink-jet plotters, and laser plotters.

raster   Grid. A raster scan CRT stores and displays data as a horizontal grid of picture cells (pixels).

real time image generation   Computations necessary to update an image completed within the refresh rate, so that a viewer receives the impression of reality. Highly complex calculations are required in applications such as flight simulation.

refresh   Rewriting of an image to the display screen to re-excite the phosphors and maintain a constant, flicker-free image.

resolution   Number of pixels per unit of area in a raster scan CRT. A display with a finer grid of more pixels is capable of reproducing more detail in an image.

software   General term for all computer programs. Software provides the communication between user and machine so that an action prompts the desired response.

telecommunication   Direct communication between two or more computer terminals or systems over telephone lines.

transformation   Mathematical routines that make it possible to rotate, scale, or otherwise manipulate an object once its coordinates are stored in memory.

vector   Line.

vector refresh CRT   Display device that stores and displays data as line segments, which are identified by the coordinates of their endpoints.

VDT   Video display terminal. A raster format display that uses an analog signal. A digital to analog converter yields the video signal used for display.

workstation   Configuration of computer equipment designed for use by one person at a time. A workstation may have a terminal connected to a large computer, or may be a "stand alone" with local processing. It generally consists of an input device, a display device, memory, and an output device.

Trade Journals

Ad Week
A/S/M Communications Inc.
820 Second Avenue
New York, NY 10017

Architectural Record
McGraw-Hill
1221 Avenue of the Americas
New York, NY 10020

Automation News
Grant Publications
115 East 23rd Street
New York, NY 10010

Audio-Visual Communications
Media Horizons
50 West 23rd Street
New York, NY 10010

AV Video
Montage Publishing Inc.
25550 Hawthorne Boulevard
Torrance, CA 90505

CAD/CAM Technology
Computer and Automated
  Systems Association of the
  Society of Manufacturing
  Engineers (CASA/SME)
One SME Drive
Dearborn, MI 48121

Communication Arts
Coyne & Blanchard Inc.
410 Sherman Avenue
Palo Alto, CA 94303

Computer Aided Engineering
Denton IPC
1111 Chester Avenue
Cleveland, OH 44114

Computer Graphics Today
Penwell Directories
P.O. Box 21278
Tulsa, OK 74121

Computer Pictures
Back Stage Publications
350 West 42nd Street
New York, NY 10036

Datamation
Technical Publishing
875 Third Avenue
New York, NY 10022

Electronic Design
Hayden Publishing Co.
10 Mulholland Drive
Hasbrouck Heights, NJ 07604

*S. Klein Newsletter on
  Computer Graphics*
Technology & Business
  Communications Inc.
730 Boston Post Road
Sudbury, MA 01776

Print
RC Publications
355 Lexington Avenue
New York, NY 10007

Appendix **C**

Societies and Associations

American Association For Medical Systems and Informatics
4405 East-West Highway
Bethesda, MD 20819

American Medical Association
535 North Dearborn Street
Chicago, IL 60610

Association for Computing Machinery's Special Interest Group
  on Computer Graphics (SIGGRAPH)
11 West 42nd Street
New York, NY 10036

Computer and Automated Systems Association of The Society
  of Manufacturing Engineers (CASA/SME)
One SME Drive
Dearborn, MI 48121

Graphic Arts Guild
30 East 20th Street
New York, NY 10003

International Graphic Arts Education Association
4615 Forbes Avenue
Pittsburgh, PA 15213

National Computer Graphics Association
2722 Merrilee Drive
Fairfax, VA 22031

Society for Computer Applications in Engineering, Planning
  and Architecture
385 Hungerford Drive
Rockville, MD 20850

Society for Computer Simulations
P.O. Box 2228
LaJolla, CA 92038

Society for Information Display
654 North Sepulveda Boulevard
Los Angeles, CA 80049

Society for Information Management
One Illinois Center
111 East Wacker Drive
Chicago, IL 60601

World Computer Graphics Association
2033 M Street
Washington, DC 20036

Appendix **D**

Colleges and Universities Offering Computer Courses

COMPUTER GRAPHICS CONCEPTS AND SYSTEMS

ALABAMA

Birmingham-Southern College
Computer Services
Birmingham, AL 35254

Jacksonville State University
Computer Science
Jacksonville, AL 36265

University of Alabama
Computer Science
University, AL 35486

University of Alabama
-Birmingham
Computer and Information
Sciences
Birmingham, AL 35294

ARIZONA

Arizona State University
Computer Science
Tempe, AZ 85287

University of Arizona
Computer Science
Tucson, AZ 85721

CALIFORNIA

California Polytechnic State
University
Computer Science/Statistics
San Luis Obispo, CA 93407

California State Polytechnic
University
Computer Science
Pomona, CA 91768

California State College
-Stanislaus
Computer Science
Turlock, CA 95380

California State University
-Chico
Computer Science
Chico, CA 95929

California State University
-Northridge
Computer Science
Northridge, CA 91330

California State University
-Sacramento
Center for Computer Aided
Design Engr.
Sacramento, CA 95819

Diablo Valley College
Computer Science
Pleasant Hill, CA 94523

Mills College
Mathematics and Computer
Science
Oakland, CA 94613

Naval Postgraduate School
Computer Science
Monterey, CA 93943

Sonoma State University
Math & Computer &
Information Science
Rohnert Park, CA 94928

Stanford University
Computer Science
Stanford, CA 94305

University of California
-Berkeley
Berkeley Computer Graphics
Laboratory
Berkeley, CA 94720

University of California
-Santa Barbara
Computer Science
Santa Barbara, CA 93106

University of California
-Santa Cruz
Computer and Information
Sciences
Santa Cruz, CA 95064

University of Santa Clara
Mathematics
Santa Clara, CA 95053

COLORADO

CIBAR Systems Institute
Colorado Springs, CO 80907

Colorado Mountain College
Computer Science/Data
Processing
Glenwood Springs, CO 81602

University of Colorado Springs
Computer Science
Colorado Springs, CO 80907

United States Air Force Academy
Computer Science
Colorado Springs, CO 80840

CONNECTICUT

Central Connecticut State
University
Applied Math/Computer Science
New Britain, CT 06050

University of Connecticut
Electrical Engr and Computer
Science
Storrs, CT 06268

DELAWARE

University of Delaware
Computer and Information
Sciences
Newark, DE 19711

DISTRICT OF COLUMBIA

Howard University
Systems and Computer Science
Washington, DC 20059

The George Washington
University
Electrical Engr and Computer
Science
Washington, DC 20052

University of DC
Electrical Engr and Computer
Science
Washington, DC 20008

FLORIDA

University of Florida
Computer and Information
Sciences
Gainesville, FL 32611

GEORGIA

Georgia Institute of Technology
Information and Computer
Science
Atlanta, GA 30332

ILLINOIS

Aurora College
Computer Science
Aurora, IL 60506

Concordia College
Computer Science
River Forest, IL 60305

Southern Illinois University
Computer Science
Carbondale, IL 62901

University of Illinois at Chicago
Electrical Engr and Computer
Science
Chicago, IL 60680

Western Illinois University
Computer Science
Macomb, IL 61455

INDIANA

Ball State University
Computer Science
Muncie, IN 47306

Indiana State University
Math/Computer Science-Physics
Terre Haute, IN 47809

Purdue University
Computer Science
West Lafayette, IN 47907

Purdue University-Calumet
Information Systems and
Computer Programming
Hammond, IN 46323

Taylor University
Information Sciences
Upland, IN 46989

Valparaiso University
Academic Computing
Valparaiso, IN 46383

IOWA

Luther College
Computer Science
Decorah, IA 52101

University of Iowa
Instructional Design-Education
Iowa City, IA 52242

Wartburg College
Mathematics & Computer
Science
Waverly, IA 50677

KENTUCKY

Eastern Kentucky University
Industrial Education &
Technology
Richmond, KY 40475

MAINE

University of Maine
Computer Science
Orono, ME 04469

MARYLAND

Essex Community College
Mathematics/Computer Science
Baltimore County, MD 21237

Goucher College
Mathematics and Computer
Science
Towson, MD 21204

Johns Hopkins University/APL
Center
Whiting School of Engineering
Baltimore, MD 21218

Salisbury State College
Computer Science
Salisbury, MD 21801

MASSACHUSETTS

Boston University
Computer Science
Boston, MA 02215

Harvard University
Aiken Computation Laboratory
Cambridge, MA 02138

Smith College
Computer Science
Northampton, MA 01063

Worcester Polytechnic Institute
Computer Science
Worcester, MA 01609

MICHIGAN

Alma College
Mathematics/Computer Science
Alma, MI 48801

Hope College
Computer Science
Holland, MI 49423

Wayne State University
Computer Science
Detroit, MI 48202

MINNESOTA

College of St. Thomas
Quantitative Methods/
Computer Science
St. Paul, MN 55105

Moorhead State University
Computer Science
Moorhead, MN 56560

St. Olaf College
Mathematics
Northfield, MN 55057

University of Minnesota
Computer Science
Minneapolis, MN 55455

University of Minnesota-Duluth
Mathematical Sciences
Duluth, MN 55812

MISSISSIPPI

Millsaps College
Computer Studies
Jackson, MS 39210

University of Mississippi
Computer Science
University, MS 38677

MISSOURI

Northwest Missouri State
University
Computer Science
Maryville, MO 64468

Rockhurst College
Mathematics & Computer
Science
Kansas City, MO 64110

NEVADA

University of Nevada
Electrical Engr and Computer
Science
Reno, NV 89557

NEW HAMPSHIRE

University of New Hampshire
Computer Science
Durham, NH 03824

NEW JERSEY

Rutgers University
Mathematical Sciences
Camden, NJ 08102

NEW MEXICO
University of New Mexico
Electrical and Computer
Engineering/Computer Science
Albuquerque, NM 87110

NEW YORK
Clarkson University
Electrical & Computer Engr/
Mathematics & Computer
Science
Potsdam, NY 13676

Cayuga Community College
Math Engineering
Auburn, NY 13021

Columbia-Greene Community
College
Science & Technology Studies
Hudson, NY 12534

Cornell University
Program of Computer Graphics
Ithaca, NY 14853

C. W. Post College of Long
Island University
Computer Science
Greenvale, NY 11548

Hobart & William Smith College
Mathematics and Computer
Science
Geneva, NY 14456

Mercy College
Mathematics/Computer Science
Dobbs Ferry, NY 10522

Mohawk Valley Community
College
Computer Science
Utica, NY 13501

Niagara University
Computer and Information
Sciences
Niagara University, NY 14109

New York University
Computer Science
New York, NY 10012

Pratt Institute
Computer Science
Brooklyn, NY 11205

Rochester Institute of Technology
Computer Science
Rochester, NY 14623

Siena College
Computer Science
Loudonville, NY 12211

SUNY Potsdam
Computer and Information
Science
Potsdam, NY 13676

Union College
Electrical Engr and Computer
Science
Schenectady, NY 12308

United States Military Academy
Geography and Computer
Science
West Point, NY 10996

NORTH CAROLINA
North Carolina State University
Computer Science
Raleigh, NC 27695

NORTH DAKOTA
North Dakota State University
Computer Science
Fargo, ND 58105

OHIO
Air Force Institute of Technology
Comp Engr and Comp Sci
Wright-Patterson AFB, OH 45433

Bowling Green State University
Computer Science
Bowling Green, OH 43403

Hiram College
Mathematical Sciences
Hiram, OH 44234

Muskingum College
Mathematics & Computer
Science
New Concord, OH 43762

Ohio State University
Engineering Graphics
Columbus, OH 43210

OREGON
Chemeketa Community College
Data Processing
Salem, OR 97309

Oregon Graduate Center
Computer Science & Engineering
Beaverton, OR 97006

Oregon Institute of Technology
Computer Systems Engineering
Klamath Falls, OR 97601

Oregon State University
Computer Science
Corvallis, OR 97330

Portland State University
Computer Science
Portland, OR 97207

University of Portland
School of Engineering
Portland, OR 97203

PENNSYLVANIA

Bryn Mawr College
Bryn Mawr, PA 19010

Bucknell University
Computer Science
Lewisburg, PA 17837

Indiana University of
Pennsylvania
Computer Science
Indiana, PA 15705

Kutztown University of
Pennsylvania
Mathematics/Computer Science
Kutztown, PA 19530

Slippery Rock University
Computer Science
Slippery Rock, PA 16057

University of Pittsburgh
Computer Science
Pittsburgh, PA 15260

University of Pittsburgh
-Johnstown
Computer Science
Johnstown, PA 15904

Wilkes College
Computer Science
Wilkes-Barre, PA 18766

RHODE ISLAND

Brown University
Computer Science
Providence, RI 02912

Providence College
Computer Science
Providence, RI 02918

SOUTH CAROLINA

Winthrop College
Business
Rock Hill, SC 29733

TENNESSEE

East Tennessee State University
Computer and Information
Science
Johnson City, TN 37614

Middle Tennessee State
University
Mathematics and Computer
Science
Murfreesboro, TN 37130

The University of the South
Mathematics and Computer
Science
Sewanee, TN 37375

University of Tennessee
Geography
Knoxville, TN 37996

University of Tennessee
-Chattanooga
Computer Science
Chattanooga, TN 37402

University of Tennessee
-Martin
Mathematics and Computer
Science
Martin, TN 38238

TEXAS

Southern Methodist University
Computer Science and
Engineering
Dallas, TX 75275

Southwest Texas State University
Computer Science
San Marcos, TX 78666

Texas Tech University
Computer Science
Lubbock, TX 79409

UTAH

Weber State College
Academic Computing
Ogden, UT 84408

VERMONT

Bennington College
Computer Science
Bennington, VT 05201

VIRGINIA

Hollins College
Computer Science
Hollins, VA 24020

University of Virginia
Electrical Engineering
Charlottesville, VA 22901

Virginia Tech
Computer Science
Blacksburg, VA 24061

WASHINGTON

Pacific Lutheran University
Mathematics and Computer
Science
Tacoma, WA 98447

St. Martin's College
Software Technology
Lacey, WA 98503

Seattle University
Software Engineering
Seattle, WA 98122

University of Washington
Computer Science
Seattle, WA 98195

Walla Walla College
Engineering
College Place, WA 99324

WEST VIRGINA

Marshall University
Computer and Information
Science
Huntington, WV 25701

Salem College
Computer Science
Salem, WV 26426

WISCONSIN

Carroll College
Computer Science
Waukesha, WI 53186

Milwaukee School of Engineering
Electrical Engr and Computer
Science
Milwaukee, WI 53201

University of Wisconsin
-Madison
Computer-Aided Engineering
Center
Madison, WI 53706

University of Wisconsin-Oshkosh
Computer Science
Oshkosh, WI 54901

CANADA
ALBERTA

University of Calgary
Computer Science
Calgary, Alta T2N 1N4

BRITISH COLUMBIA

Simon Fraser University
Computing Science
Burnaby, BC V5A 1S6

University of British Columbia
Computer Science, Electrical
Engineering
Vancouver, BC V6T 1W5

MANITOBA

Brandon University
Mathematics and Computer
Science
Brandon, Man R7A 6A9

NEW BRUNSWICK

University of New Brunswick
Computer Science
Fredericton, NB E3B 5A3

NEWFOUNDLAND

Memorial University of
Newfoundland
Computer Science
St. Johns, Nfld A1B 3X7

NOVA SCOTIA

Acadia University
Computer Science
Wolfville, NS B0P 1X0

ONTARIO

Brock University
Computer Science
St. Catharines, ON L2S 3A1

University of Ottawa
Computer Science
Ottawa, Ont K1N 6N5

University of Waterloo
Computer Science
Waterloo, Ont N2L 3G1

The University of Western
Ontario
Computer Science
London, Ont N6A 5B7

York University
Computer Science
Downsview, Ont M3J 2R3

QUEBEC

Ecole Polytechnique of Montreal
CACAD
Montreal, Que H3C 3A4

McGill University
Electrical Engineering
Montreal, Que H3A 2A7

Universite de Montreal
Informatique et Recherche
Operationelle
Montreal, Que H3C 3J7

SASKATCHEWAN

University of Saskatchewan
Computational Science
Saskatoon, Sask S7N 0W0

OTHER
AUSTRALIA

University of Sydney
Basser Department of Computer
Science
Sydney, NSW 2006

P.R.C.

Tsinghua University
Computer Engineering and
  Science
Beijing

U.K.

Glasgow University
Computing Science
Glasgow, Scotland G12 8RZ

COMPUTER GRAPHICS IN ENGINEERING, CAD/CAM, AND DRAFTING

ARIZONA

Maricopa Technical College
Drafting
Phoenix, AZ 85013

University of Arizona
Aerospace & Mechanical
  Engineering
Tucson, AZ 85721

CALIFORNIA

California State University
  -Northridge
Engineering & Computer Science
Northridge, CA 91330

Mt. San Antonio College
Drafting & Design
Walnut, CA 91789

Orange Coast College
Technology
Costa Mesa, CA 92626

San Diego State University
Engineering
San Diego, CA 92182

University of California-Davis
Mechanical Engineering
Davis, CA 95616

COLORADO

Colorado State University
Center for Computer Assisted
  Engineering
Ft. Collins, CO 80523

University of Colorado-Boulder
Civil, Environmental, &
  Architectural Engineering
Boulder, CO 80309

GEORGIA

Dalton Junior College
Vo-Tech Drafting & Design
Dalton, GA 30720

IDAHO

University of Idaho
Engineering Science
Moscow, ID 83843

INDIANA

Indiana Institute of Technology
Engineering
Ft. Wayne, IN 46803

Indiana State University
School of Technology
Terre Haute, IN 47809

Purdue University
CADLAB
West Lafayette, IN 47907

Tri-State University
Drafting and Design Technology
Angola, IN 46703

Vincennes University
Drafting
Vincennes, IN 47591

IOWA

Iowa State University
Engineering
Ames, IA 50011

KANSAS

Hutchinson Community College
Computer Science
Hutchinson, KS 67501

MAINE

University of Maine-Orono
Civil Engineering & Surveying
  Engineering
Orono, ME 04469

MARYLAND

Essex Community College
Physics, Engineering, and
  Technology
Baltimore County, MD 21237

Hagerstown Junior College
Mechanical Engineering
  Technology
Hagerstown, MD 21740

Montgomery College
Engineering Technologies
Rockville, MD 20850

United States Naval Academy
Aerospace Engineering
Annapolis, MD 21402

University of Maryland
Mechanical Engineering
College Park, MD 20742

MASSACHUSETTS

Worcester Polytechnic Institute
Computer Science
Worcester, MA 01609

MICHIGAN

Eastern Michigan University
Industrial Technology
Ypsilanti, MI 48197

Muskegon Community College
Drafting Technology
Muskegon, MI 49442

University of Detroit
CAD/CAM Center
Detroit, MI 48221

Western Michigan University
Engineering Technology
Kalamazoo, MI 49008

MINNESOTA

University of Minnesota
Mechanical Engineering
Minneapolis, MN 55455

MONTANA

Montana College of Mineral
Science and Technology
Mining
Butte, MT 59701

NEVADA

University of Nevada
Electrical Engr & Computer
Science
Reno, NV 89557

NEW YORK

Broome Community College
CAD/CAM Center
Binghamton, NY 13902

Clarkson University
Mechanical & Industrial
Engineering
Potsdam, NY 13676

Rochester Institute of Technology
Drafting Technology
Rochester, NY 14614

University of Rochester
Electrical Engineering
Rochester, NY 14627

NORTH CAROLINA

Appalachian State University
Industrial Education &
Technology
Boone, NC 28608

Western Carolina University
Industrial Education &
Technology
Cullowhee, NC 28723

Wilson County Technical
Institute
Technical & Business
Wilson, NC 27893

OHIO

Ohio Northern University
Mechanical Engineering
Ada, OH 45810

Ohio State University
Engineering Graphics
Columbus, OH 43210

Ohio State University
Industrial Design
Columbus, OH 43210

University of Akron
Engineering Computer Graphics
Facility
Akron, OH 44325

OKLAHOMA

Oklahoma State University
Mechanical & Aerospace
Engineering
Stillwater, OK 74078

OREGON

University of Portland
Engineering
Portland, OR 97203

PENNSYLVANIA

Lehigh County Community
College
Mechanical Drafting & Design
Tech
Schnecksville, PA 18078

Pittsburgh Technical Institute
Computer Technologies Center
Pittsburgh, PA 15222

RHODE ISLAND

University of Rhode Island
Mechanical Engineering &
  Applied Mechanics
Kingston, RI 02881

SOUTH DAKOTA

South Dakota State University
General Engineering
Brookings, SD 57007

TEXAS

North Harris County College
Drafting
Houston, TX 77073

Paris Junior College
Drafting Technology
Paris, TX 75460

Texas Tech University
Computer Science
Lubbock, TX 79409

University of Houston
  -Downtown
Engineering & Technology
Houston, TX 77002

University of Houston
  -University Park
Civil Technology
Houston, TX 77004

UTAH

Brigham Young University
Civil Engineering
Provo, UT 84602

Weber State College
Academic Computing
Ogden, UT 84408

Weber State College
Manufacturing Engineering
  Technology
Ogden, UT 84408

VIRGINIA

University of Virginia
Electrical Engineering
Charlottesville, VA 22901

University of Virginia
Mechanical Engineering
Charlottesville, VA 22901

Virginia Institute of Technology
CAD
Norfolk, VA 23513

WEST VIRGINIA

Salem College
Computer Science
Salem, WV 26426

WISCONSIN

Milwaukee School of Engineering
Electrical Engr/Computer
  Science
Milwaukee, WI 53201

North Central Technical Institute
Technical
Wausau, WI 54401

WYOMING

University of Wyoming
Engineering
Laramie, WY 82071

CANADA

ALBERTA

University of Calgary
Electrical Engineering
Calgary, Alta T2N 1N4

QUEBEC

Ecole Polytechnique de Montreal
CACAD
Montreal, Que H3C 3A4

Univ du Quebec a Trois-Rivieres
Industrial Engineering
Trois-Rivieres, Que G9A 5H7

COMPUTER GRAPHICS IN THE ARTS, ARCHITECTURE, AND DESIGN

ARIZONA

Phoenix College
Art
Phoenix, AZ 85013

CALIFORNIA

Academy of Art College
Graphic Design/Computer
  Graphics
San Francisco, CA 94108

California College of Arts and
  Crafts
Computer Graphics Support
  Group
Oakland, CA 94618

California Institute of the Arts,
Film & Video
Valencia, CA 91355

California State Polytechnic
  University
Architecture
Pomona, CA 91768

California State University-Chico
Computer Science
Chico, CA 95929

California State University
-Long Beach
Visual Communication Design
Long Beach, CA 90840

California State University
-Northridge
Computer Science
Northridge, CA 91330

California State University
-Los Angeles
Art
Los Angeles, CA 90032

California State University
-Sacramento
Art
Sacramento, CA 95819

Chapman College
Art
Orange, CA 92666

Orange Coast College
Computer Graphics/Fine Arts
Costa Mesa, CA 92626

Pacific Basin School of
Textile Arts
Berkeley, CA 94702

Santa Ana College
Art
Santa Ana, CA 92706

West Coast University
Computer Graphics for Artists
& Designers
Los Angeles, CA 90020

COLORADO

University of Colorado
Fine Arts
Boulder, CO 80309

CONNECTICUT

Central Connecticut State
University
Applied Mathematics/
Computer Science
New Britain, CT 06050

ILLINOIS

Illinois Institute of Technology
Institute of Design
Chicago, IL 60616

Northern Illinois University
Art
DeKalb, IL 60115

Prairie State College
Visual Communication
Chicago Heights, IL 60411

Southern Illinois University
Commercial Graphic Design
Carbondale, IL 62918

The School of the Art Institute
of Chicago
Art and Technology
Chicago, IL 60603

INDIANA

Purdue University-Calumet
Communication
Hammond, IN 46323

IOWA

Drake University
Media Graphics
Des Moines, IA 50311

Mount Mercy College
Art
Cedar Rapids, IA 52402

KANSAS

University of Kansas
Design & Industrial Design
Lawrence, KS 66045

LOUISIANA

Louisiana State University
Architecture/Interior Design/
Landscape Architecture/Art
Baton Rouge, LA 70803

University of Louisiana
Architecture
Lafayette, LA 70504

MARYLAND

Maryland Institute College of Art
Visual Communication
Baltimore, MD 21217

Montgomery College
Computer Science/Art
Rockville, MD 20814

MASSACHUSETTS

Massachusetts College of Art
Boston, MA 02115

Smith College
Art
Northampton, MA 01063

The New England School of Art
and Design
Graphic Design
Boston, MA 02116

MINNESOTA

Minneapolis College of Art and
Design
Design Division
Minneapolis, MN 55404

MISSOURI
Kansas City Art Institute
Design
Kansas City, MO 64111

University of Missouri
Housing & Interior Design
Columbia,MO 65211

MONTANA
Western Montana College
Art
Dillon, MT 59725

NEW JERSEY
Kean College of New Jersey
Fine Arts
Union, NJ 07083

NEW YORK
Buffalo State College
Design
Buffalo, NY 14222

Fashion Institute of Technology
Computer Graphics
New York, NY 10001

Hofstra University
Fine Arts
Hempstead, NY 11550

New York Institute of Technology
Center for Architecture
Old Westbury, NY 11568

Rensselaer Polytechnic Institute
Architecture
Troy, NY 12181

Rochester Inst of Technology/
  Natl Institute for the Deaf
Applied Art
Rochester, NY 14623

Rochester Institute of Technology
Fine and Applied Arts
Rochester, NY 14623

School of Visual Arts
Computer Graphics
New York, NY 10010

Syracuse University
Art Media Studies
Syracuse, NY 13210

NORTH CAROLINA
North Carolina State Dept of
  Public Instruction
State Art Consultant
Raleigh, NC 27611

OHIO
Bowling Green State University
Art
Bowling Green, OH 43403

Columbus College of Art and
  Design
Industrial Design
Columbus, OH 43215

Ohio State University
Computer Graphics Research
  Group
Columbus, OH 43201

Ohio State University
Industrial Design
Columbus, OH 43210

OKLAHOMA
Oklahoma State Tech
Graphic Arts
Okmulgee, OK 74447

OREGON
Mt. Hood Community College
Visual Art
Gresham, OR 97030

University of Oregon
Fine and Applied Art/
  Architecture
Eugene, OR 97403

PENNSYLVANIA
Art Institute of Philadelphia
Commercial Art
Philadelphia, PA 19103

Moore College of Art
Philadelphia, PA 19103

RHODE ISLAND
Rhode Island College
Art
Providence, RI 02911

SOUTH DAKOTA
Northern State College
Art
Aberdeen, SD 57401

South Dakota State University
Visual Arts
Brookings, SD 57007

TEXAS
Baylor University
Fine Arts
Waco, TX 76798

North Texas State University
Art
Denton, TX 76203

Texas Womans University
Advertising/Art
Denton, TX 76203

UTAH
Weber State College
Academic Computing
Ogden, UT 84408

VERMONT
Green Mt. College
Art
Poultney, VT 05764

VIRGINIA
James Madison University
Art
Harrisonburg, VA 22807

University of Virginia
Architecture
Charlottesville, VA 22901

Virginia Commonwealth
University
Communications Arts & Design
Richmond, VA 23284

WASHINGTON
Washington State University
Architecture
Pullman, WA 99164

WISCONSIN
Milwaukee Institute of Art and
Design
Milwaukee, WI 53202

University of Wisconsin-Madison
Art
Madison, WI 53706

CANADA
ONTARIO
Durham College
Graphic Design
Oshawa, Ont L1H 7L7

Mohawk College of Applied
Arts and Technology
Television Broadcasting
Hamilton, Ont L8N 3T2

Sheridan College
Computer Graphics Laboratory
Oakville, Ont L6H 2L1

QUEBEC
College du Vieux-Montreal
Design
Beloeil, Que J3G 2C9

Universite de Montreal
Informatique et Recherche
Operationelle
Montreal, Que H3C 3J7

COMPUTER GRAPHICS IN GEOGRAPHY
AND GEOLOGY

ALABAMA
Jacksonville State University
Geography
Jacksonville, AL 36265

ARIZONA
Arizona State University
Geography
Tempe, AZ 85287

CALIFORNIA
California State University
-Fresno
Geography
Fresno, CA 93740

Humboldt State University
Geography
Arcata, CA 95521

University of California
-Los Angeles
Geography
Los Angeles, CA 90024

CONNECTICUT
Central Connecticut State
University
Geography
New Britain, CT 06050

Southern Connecticut State
University
Geography
New Haven, CT 06515

FLORIDA
Florida State University
Geography
Tallahassee, FL 32306

University of Florida
Geography
Gainesville, FL 32605

GEORGIA
Georgia State University
Geography
Atlanta, GA 30303

ILLINOIS

Augustana College
Physics
Rock Island, IL 61201

DePaul University
Geography
Chicago, IL 60614

Eastern Illinois University
Geography & Geology
Charleston, IL 61920

University of Illinois
Geography
Urbana, IL 61801

INDIANA

Indiana State University
Geography & Geology
Terre Haute, IN 47809

Indiana University-Purdue
University-Indianapolis
Geography
Indianapolis, IN 46202

IOWA

University of Northern Iowa
Geography
Cedar Falls, IA 50614

KENTUCKY

Western Kentucky University
Geography & Geology
Bowling Green, KY 42101

MARYLAND

Frostburg State College
Geography
Frostburg, MD 21532

MASSACHUSETTS

Smith College
Geology
Northampton, MA 01063

MICHIGAN

Central Michigan University
Geography
Mt. Pleasant, MI 48859

Northern Michigan University
Geography & Planning
Marquette, MI 49855

Western Michigan University
Geography
Kalamazoo, MI 49008

MINNESOTA

University of Minnesota-Duluth
Sociology/Anthropology/
Geography
Duluth, MN 55812

MISSOURI

University of Missouri
-Columbia
Geography
Columbia, MO 65201

NEVADA

University of Nevada-Reno
Geography
Reno, NV 89557

NEW YORK

SUNY-Geneseo
Geography
Geneseo, NY 14454

Syracuse University
Geography
Syracuse, NY 13210

The College at New Paltz, SUNY
Geography
New Paltz, NY 12561

United States Military Academy
Geography & Computer Science
West Point, NY 10996

NORTH CAROLINA

Appalachian State University
Community Planning &
Geography
Boone, NC 28608

East Carolina University
Geography & Planning
Greenville, NC 27834

OHIO

Ohio State University
Geography
Columbus, OH 43210

University of Akron
Geography
Akron, OH 44325

OKLAHOMA

University of Oklahoma
Geography
Norman, OK 73019

TENNESSEE

Memphis State University
Geography and Planning
Memphis, TN 38152

University of Tennessee
Geography
Knoxville, TN 37996

TEXAS

Texas A&M University
Geography
College Station, TX 77843

University of Texas-Austin
Geography
Austin, TX 78712

VIRGINIA

Radford University
Geography
Radford, VA 24142

Virginia Tech
Geography
Blacksburg, VA 24061

WISCONSIN

University of Wisconsin
-Eau Claire
Geography
Eau Claire, WI 54701

University of Wisconsin
-Madison
Geography & Cartography
Madison, WI 53706

University of Wisconsin
-Whitewater
Geography
Whitewater, WI 53190

WYOMING

University of Wyoming
Geography
Laramie, WY 82071

CANADA
ALBERTA

University of Alberta
Geography
Edmonton, Alta T6G 2H4

University of Calgary
Geography
Calgary, Alta T2N 1N4

BRITISH COLUMBIA

University of Victoria
Geography
Victoria, BC V8W 2Y2

ONTARIO

University of Western Ontario
Geography
London, Ont N6A 5C2

University of Windsor
Geography
Windsor, Ont N9B 3P4

SASKATCHEWAN

University of Saskatchewan
Geography
Saskatoon, Sask S7N 0W0

COMPUTER GRAPHICS IN GENERAL
AND BUSINESS APPLICATIONS

CALIFORNIA

California Polytechnic State
  University
Computer Science & Statistics
San Luis Obispo, CA 93407

California State Polytechnic
  University
Computer Information Systems
Pomona, CA 91768

California State University
  -Northridge
Computer Science
Northridge, CA 91330

Golden West College
Business, Health & Applied
  Science
Huntington Beach, CA 92647

San Francisco State University
Information Science
San Francisco, CA 94132

COLORADO

Western State College
Computer Science
Gunnison, CO 81230

CONNECTICUT

Central Connecticut State
  University
Applied Math & Computer
  Science
New Britain, CT 06050

DELAWARE

Goldey Bascom College
Business Information Systems
Wilmington, DE 19808

GEORGIA

Georgia State University
Geography
Atlanta, GA 30303

ILLINOIS

Augustana College
Physics Department
Rock Island, IL 61201

Concordia College
Computer Science
River Forest, IL 60305

Western Illinois University
Computer Science
Macomb, IL 61455

KANSAS

Hutchinson Community College
Computer Science
Hutchinson, KS 67501

MARYLAND

Montgomery College
Computer Science
Rockville, MD 20814

MISSOURI

Southwest Missouri State
  University
Computer Information Systems
Springfield, MO 65802

NEW YORK

School of Visual Arts
Computer Graphics
New York, NY 10010

OHIO

Xavier University
Information & Decision Sciences
Cincinnati, OH 45207

TEXAS

Grayson County College
Business Division
Denison, TX 75020

WEST VIRGINIA

Salem College
Computer Science
Salem, WV 26426

BIBLIOGRAPHY

Angell, I.O. *A Practical Introduction to Computer Graphics*. New York: Halsted Press, 1981.

Bolles, Richard. *What Color Is Your Parachute?* Berkeley: Ten Speed Press, 1986.

Foley, J.D., and A. van Dam. *Fundamentals of Interactive Computer Graphics*. Reading, MA: Addison Wesley, 1981.

Greenburg, Donald. *The Computer Image*. Reading, MA: Addison Wesley, 1982.

Leavitt, R., ed. *Artist and Computer*. New York: Harmony Books, 1976.

Newman, W.N., and R.F. Sproull. *Principles of Interactive Computer Graphics* (2nd ed.). New York: McGraw–Hill, 1979.

Paetro, Maxine. *How to Put Your Book Together and Get a Job in Advertising*. New York: E.P. Dutton & Co., 1980.

Parslow, R.D., et al, eds. *Computer Graphics: Techniques and Applications*. New York: Plenum Press, 1975.

Scott, J.E. *Introduction to Interactive Computer Graphics*. New York: John Wiley & Sons, 1982.

Schmid, C.F. and S.E. *Handbook of Graphic Presentations*. New York: John Wiley & Sons, 1979.

Waite, M. *Computer Graphics Primer*. Indianapolis: Howard W. Sams & Co. Inc., 1979.

Weintraub, Joseph. *Exploring Careers in the Computer Field*. New York: Rosen Publishing Group, 1983.

Index

A

Abel, Robert & Associates, 4
ads, classified, 24, 28
Advertising
  computer graphics applications in,
    53, 55
  television, 4
aggressiveness, 11-13
air brush, 56
alphanumerics, 41, 43
American Academy of Ophthalmology,
  46
American Can Council, 3
animation, 8, 13, 39, 79, 81-82
  computer graphics applications in,
    56-58, 82, 88
  full-scale, 6, 44, 82, 111
  of human body, 69
  inbetweeners, 13, 57
  structural, 118-128
applications, computer graphics, 6, 7,
  16, 17, 18-19, 20, 53-78
architecture, 5, 6, 7, 8, 11, 14, 39, 43,
  61, 62-65, 66
  career ladder, 63
art
  computer-graphic applications, 40,
    51, 53-56, 109
  fine, 8, 55, 103, 116
  student, 112-113
  video, 44
artificial intelligence, 125
artist, 11, 72, 76
  graphic, 79, 90-91, 97-107
  pasteup, 13
  video, 13
Association for Computing Machinery,
  28

B

backache, 46, 47, 48
Bell Laboratories, 34
body copy, 131
Bressler, Martin, 6, 12-13, 108-117
Brilliant Image, 5, 96-107
business, 6, 14
  career ladder, 70
  computer graphics applications in,

51, 70-76, 111
microcomputer in, 40, 42, 96-107
owning, 11

C

CAD/CAM, 7, 8, 12, 13-14, 41
  computer graphics applications,
    51-52, 61-76
Cahn, Jerry, 5, 96-107
camera system, color, 37
cardiac problem, 45, 46, 47
career
  in computer graphics, 10-14
  in or with computers, 7
  goals, 15, 16, 32
  ladder, 54
  opportunities, 9, 31, 52, 61, 74-75, 93,
    103-104, 127-128
cartoon, 8, 57
cathode ray tube (CRT), 34, 45-48
central processing unit (CPU), 34, 35
chalk, 56
chart, 5, 6, 7, 8, 40, 64, 72, 75, 82
  bar, 7, 13, 34, 74, 101
  pie, 34
chemistry, 58, 61, 68
  career ladder in, 63
color, 105, 120
  copy, 37
  electron gun, 39
  inputting, 57
communication, 7, 8, 14, 64, 87, 97,
  105-106, 123, 129
  business, 29
  machine/user, 33, 35-36
  telecommunication, 67
  visual, 11
computer, 11, 13, 16, 132-133
  mainframe, 40
  mini, 40, 109
  simulation, 43
  time, 12, 48, 115, 117
computer-aided design (CAD), 7, 14,
  140, 41, 52, 68, 72, 111, 120
computer-aided engineering, 66-67,
  111, 120, 121, 127
computer-aided learning (CAL), 41, 42
computer-aided manufacturing (CAM),

7, 67, 120
Computer and Business Equipment
  Manufacturers Association
  (CBEMA), 45, 46
Concourse Engineering Co., 5
contacts, making, 16, 20, 28, 31
copy
  color, 37
  hard, 42, 43
cover letter, 22-27, 30
creativity, 6, 11, 17, 43, 55, 65, 66, 76,
  80, 92, 103, 124
  in cover letter, 26-27, 30
cursor, 36, 55

D
data
  analysis, 72, 74, 119-120
  input, 33, 55, 64
  management, 40
  processor, 43
  storage, 34
database, 43, 67
deadline, 82, 83
  production, 14, 48
decision support, 5, 8, 40, 72-73,
  75
design
  advertising art, 7, 8
  architectural, 63-65
  commercial, 55
  computer, 129-133
  computer graphics applications, 5,
    11, 53, 55, 72
  engineering, 14
  graphics, 109
  interior, 8, 64, 111
  manufacturing, 14
  package, 8
  structural, 66, 120
  technical, 43, 124-125
    traditional, 130-132
desktop publishing, 129-133
digitizer, 55
direct view storage tube CRT, 35, 38, 39
display device, 36, 38, 44
drafting, computer graphics, 5, 64, 72
draftsmen, architectural, 13, 14
drawings
  computer, 14, 33, 120, 131
  perspective, 64
drum plotter, 37

Dubner animation system, 6, 79, 81, 85,
  86

E
education, 15, 17
  computer, 12, 18, 106, 133
  computer graphics in, 68, 69
  early childhood, 41
  microcomputer in, 42
educator, interview with, 108-117
electrostatic plotter, 37
engineer, 8, 14
  analytical, interview with, 118-128
  graphic design, 79-95
engineering, 5, 6, 11, 39, 43, 52, 58, 61,
  62, 66-68, 72
  CAE, 66, 67
  career ladder, 63
entrepreneur, 11, 40-41, 93
  interview with, 96-107
experience
  interviewing, 31
  job, 16-17, 19, 20, 62, 92
  system-specific, 17, 18
eyestrain, 46, 47, 48

F
Facsimile, 129
film recorder, color, 37
flat-bed plotter, 37
font, type, 56

G
General Motors, 5, 34
GenRad, 118
graph, 7, 8, 34, 37, 40, 51, 55, 64, 72,
  74, 75
Graphical Kernel System (GKS), 35
Grass Valley Switcher, 82, 85

H
Haffey, Sam Anson, 5
handicapped, 41-42
hardware, 9, 34, 35, 36, 40, 42, 48, 97,
  109, 125
health, and computer grahics, 45-48, 83
Henrickson, Ernie, 6, 79-95
histogram, 34
hours, of work, 16, 83, 127

I
illustration, 7, 8, 130-132
image
  color, 40

controllable, 39
generation, 52, 58-60, 108-109
graphics, 41
steady, 35, 38, 39
storage of, 33
three-dimensional, 34
imaging
full-scale, 57-58
three-dimensional, 57
industry
analyst, 7
computer graphics, 16, 68, 72
ink-jet plotter, color, 37, 38
input device, 36
interactive computer graphics, 3, 33, 34,
68, 91
interface, computer/user, 35, 125-126
internship, 18, 19, 103-104, 106
interview
exploratory, 29, 30
job, 16, 27, 30-32
live, 29, 30, 31
questions in, 31

J
job
-costing, 67
first, 13
how to look for, 28-30
ladder, 52, 53, 61, 63, 70
market, 9
part-time/summer, 19
where to look for, 27-28
joystick, 36, 43, 55

K
Ketchum Advertising, 4

L
light pen, 36, 38
Linotron machine, 132
local area network (LAN), 42, 43
gateway, 43
Lockheed Aircraft, 34

M
Macintosh, 133
major, double, 18
managers, 43, 71-72, 74-75
contacting, 30
Maleci, Giulio, 118-128
manipulation, of elements, 34, 36, 57,
59, 64, 111

manufacturing, computer graphics, 5, 6,
72, 120
map, 6, 9, 66, 73, 74, 75, 82
colored-coded, 4, 7
marker comp, 131
marketing, 73-74, 122
Massachusetts Institute of Technology,
34
matrix printer, color, 37, 38
McAlpin, Edward, 12
mechanical, 131
medicine, 8, 18, 58, 68-69
memory
bubble, 94
computer, 34, 35, 36, 37, 58, 116
IBM PC, 40
microcomputer, 5, 9, 35, 75, 96-107, 109
and the future, 40-44
microprocessor, 35, 119
minor, interdisciplinary, 18
mobility
job, 16, 20, 84, 101, 126
programmer, 35
mouse, 36, 55, 130, 131, 133

N
National Computer Graphics
Association (NCGA), 28
National Institute for Occupational
Safety and Health (NIOSH), 48
negatives, avoiding, 24, 32
network, computer, 67-68
New York Institute of Technology, 6,
12, 108-117
9 to 5, 45

O
obsolescence, of knowledge, 12, 71
Olsen, Millie, 4
output device, 36, 37

P
Paint Box, 6, 55-56, 79, 80, 81, 85, 86,
114
Pepsico, 4
personal computer (PC), 40, 72, 97,
114, 119
pixel, 39
portfolio, 30, 53, 89, 92, 99, 113,
114-115
and résumé, 26, 104
presentations, 6, 8, 11, 40, 69, 72-73,
75, 96, 97, 100, 105

pressure
job, 16, 127
time, 12, 47, 48, 52, 85
printer, laser, 129
productivity, 13, 14, 43, 52, 71, 73, 74
professional societies, 28
prototype, testing, 121, 125-126
publishing, 53, 55

Q
Quantel, 6, 55, 114

R
raster scan CRT, 35, 38, 39
research, 34, 41, 58, 68, 124
resolution, screen, 39, 103, 116, 119
résumé, 16-23, 29, 92, 104, 115
and creative cover letter, 26
rewards, personal/financial, 3, 11, 15
rotation, 34, 36, 59, 64

S
SAGE, 34
salary, 84
future, 16
information, 25
ladder, 52, 53, 62, 63, 70-71
scaling, 34, 36, 64
scanning, 131
school
choosing, 17, 102, 106-107
graduate, 18, 113, 114
science, 43
computer, 18
physical, 41
semiconductor chip, 35
service bureau, computer, 100
Service Employees International Union
(SEIU), 45
shading, 56, 64
Shen, Richard, 129-133
simulation, 58-60
fighter, 6, 58
flight, 7, 34, 60
ship, 59-60
skills
job, 9
technical, 41, 89
typing, 20, 42
slide, 5, 7, 8, 55
presentation, 6, 8, 96, 101, 114, 122
show, 97-98
software, 9, 36, 40, 64, 97, 103, 109, 121

database management, 67
standardization of, 35
special effects, 8, 44, 55, 56, 101
specs, type, 131
staff, graphic arts, 13-14, 35
stress
analysis, 66, 69
personal, 47, 48, 52, 82-83
Sutherland, Ivan E., 34
system
ADDA, 79, 81, 84, 91
bismo, 79
computer graphic, 5, 17, 24
Images, 109, 112
paint, 40

T
tablet, 36, 40, 55
teaching, 11, 41
technology
computer, 12, 13, 17, 33-39, 71-72,
129-132
microcomputer, 40
television, 39
television
animations, 8, 56-57
computer graphics applications in,
53, 55
testing, structural, 118-128
thumbnail, 130
Time Engineering, 12
Toby, Michael M., 5
tool
computer as, 6, 7, 55, 65, 73, 76, 109,
110, 117
obsolescence of, 85, 128
trackball, 36-37
trade, journals, 16, 17, 28, 30, 106
Transamerica, 4
translation, 34, 36
TRW, 4
type, computer, 131

U
union, 81, 90
Unlimited Grafix Ink, 129

V
Vannier, Michael, 6
vector refresh CRT, 34, 35, 38, 39
video (*see also* Television)
game, 42, 43
input, 56

interface to computer, 13, 111
video display terminal (VDT), and
   health, 45-48

W
wash, 56

wide-area network (WAN), 43
women
   in computer graphics, 93, 101
   pregnant, and VDT, 34, 46, 48
workstation, computer graphics, 40, 52,
   97, 100, 123, 128